I0192496

Poems by the Skunk River Valley Boys

Barry and Steve Benson

BLUE LIGHT PRESS ◆ 1ST WORLD PUBLISHING

1st WORLD
PUBLISHING

SAN FRANCISCO ◆ FAIRFIELD ◆ DELHI

POEMS BY THE SKUNK RIVER VALLEY BOYS

Copyright ©2015 by Barry and Steve Benson

All rights reserved. Printed in the United States of America. No part of this book may be used or reproduced in any manner whatsoever without written permission except in the case of brief quotations embodied in critical articles and reviews. For information contact:

1ST WORLD LIBRARY
PO Box 2211
Fairfield, Iowa 52556
www.1stworldpublishing.com

BLUE LIGHT PRESS
www.bluelightpress.com
Email: bluelightpress@aol.com

COVER AND BOOK DESIGN
Melanie Gendron
www.melaniegendron.com

COVER AND INTERIOR PHOTOGRAPHS
Mike Jensen

FIRST EDITION

LIBRARY OF CONGRESS CONTROL NUMBER: 2015904294

ISBN 9781421837284

DEDICATIONS

BARRY'S:

To Sally, Cory, Mark, Josef, Daniel, Sam, Kirsten.

To my writing group: Dee DePhillips and Linda Stober.

And to my mentors: Professor Dwight C. Marsh and Professor George F. Day.

STEVE'S:

To Darla, Reid, Chloe and Logan.

To Jennie and Arnold who took me home even though I didn't look a bit like my brother!

To my generous classmates, trusting teammates, patient teachers and encouraging coaches.

Special thanks to cousins Elizabeth and Kathy for all those breathless minutes in the magical "playhouse" where the poetry started.

To Mike and Patsy Jensen for all their help with this book, including the photo on the cover, the fun title, and even a good recipe for Kringla!

Also to my cribbage-playing partners Jim & Jules, Stuie Craig, Denny Keith, and Stevie Ray.

Lastly, to my brother Barry—friend, adviser (whether I wanted to listen or not) and confidant since birth who could always throw a tighter spiral with a football, hit those high fast pitches in baseball, swish the long jumper from the top of the key in basketball, and color with crayons way better than I ever could.

ACKNOWLEDGMENTS

Thanks to the editors of the following journals in which many of these poems first appeared, some in earlier versions, or under different titles:

Antioch Review: "Aunt Clara Writes."

Barbaric Yawp: "Dad," "Somewhere Over The Atlantic."

Blue Unicorn: "A Blue Heron," "A Close Call," "And Slowly Pulled."

Brevities: "A One-point Perspective," "Bella," "Mid-Winter & Late Winter," "Old Man Racing Spring," "Orange-Yellow Hunter's Moon," "Red-Wings Return," "The Last Guest," "Writing Class Protege."

BriarCliff Review: "Last Gas Station Before The Desert," "Rhabdomancy."

Bryant Literary Review: "Sonny."

Chaffin Journal: "Claiming a First," "Crusin' Dead On," "Dancing in a Golden Tent," "Fishing for Pigs," "17," "Sun," "Teaching My Mother How to Smoke."

Christian Science Monitor: "In a Hard Wind," "Straight."

Common Ground Review: "Villa Nelle Cemetery Plot Homonyms: A Magazine Found in Every Rifle."

Comstock Review: "Epiphany of Melancholy Wanderers."

Creosote: "Buddy Holly Ghazal," "Father & Son & Football," "Feeding the Queen," "Meadowlark, Goldfinch, Spring Musical," "My Father's Hammer," "Premonition," "0600 Reveille," "River Horse."

Daily Palette—Iowa Writes Online: "Crossing Iowa by Car," "Poem to be Read at 3 p.m."

Delta Epsilon Sigma Journal (of the National Catholic Honor Society): "Apple Capsule."

Descant: "Benson Tersely Toes the Rubber."

First Water—Best of Pirene's Fountain Anthology, Volume 1: "Damselfly."

Iodine Poetry Journal: "Herb's Room," "New Day Eyes," "Out of Nowhere."

The Kerf: "A Former Bowler Finds a Muddy Bird's Nest . . ."

Lyrical Iowa: "To Ann, My Student of Writing & Mythology," "Gasping On the Beach of Chance," "Gliding," "Having and Holding."

Minnesota Review: "Good of Him."

Mudfish: "Pissing Beside Donald Hall," "She Worked Part-Time to Help Out."

Nerve Cowboy: "Channels."

New Laurel Review: "Finding a Spiritual Guide in a Bar Off Bourbon."

New Orphic Review: "Father, Son, & Ruth Harmon."

Nomad's Choir: "A Pirate's Profile."

North American Review: "Norwegian Funeral," "The."

Plainsongs: "Measured Evidence," "Our Dad," "Paul's Ox," "Police Use Taser in Local Poet's Arrest," and "Shooting Hoops With Adlai."

Poem: "The Sweater."

Poet & Critic: "A Mystery."

Raw Dog Post Poem: "Old Blood in Oslo."

River Oak Review: "Found Poem—in Response to an Editor's Query," "Marginal Comments," "Measured Evidence."

Slant: "At the 1961 Ankeny Relays," "Distant Thunder," "Mike & Mike," "Rusty Equipment," "Tunnel of Tin."

Snowy Egret: "The First Fly."

Sonora Review: "San Diego Drydock," "Spaghett Whistling to Those Birds," "Yeoman's Reveille."

South Carolina Review: "My Father's Silver Dollars."

Thin Air: "A Navy Vet of Adak, Agattu, Amchitka Atu, Kiska."

Timber Creek Review: "A Nap in Shakespeare's Cap," "A One-Point Perspective," "The Sinking of the Edmund Fitzgerald."

Triton Press: "A Good Cremation," "Kathy."

Weber – The Contemporary West: "We."

Wild Violet: "Run Down by a Dune Buggy on Fire Island."

Willard & Maple: "The Big Can Theory."

Writer's Journal: "Languages and Oranges."

CONTENTS

POEMS BY THE SKUNK RIVER VALLEY BOYS

~~~

"What the river says, that is what I say."
—William Stafford

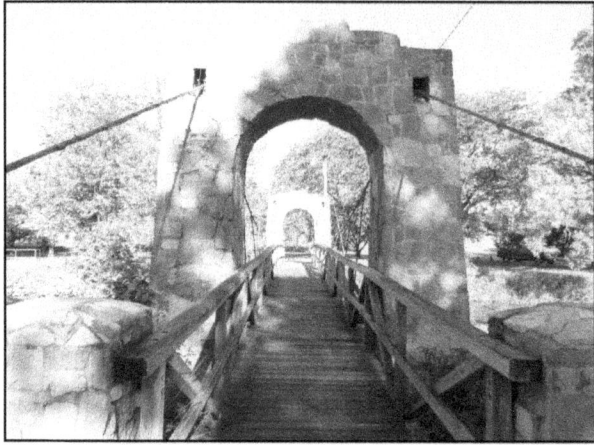

MAYOR MIKE OF TREE CITY

Roasted at a Hometown Poetry Reading

Today he is the mayor—sixty years ago he was one
of Story City's delinquents throwing water balloons
at specially selected cars and trucks from rooftop
vantage points of the town's Main Street businesses.
Saturday nights he was one of us armed with straws
and dry Navy beans purchased at the Pioneer Store
who probably horrified innocent shoppers. Friday
nights, he will admit, he was one of those in the back
rows at The Story Theater who dumped Boston Baked
Beans to roll all the way down to the very front row.

You've probably heard him tell the story, many times,
of when he and others of us tested the theory that on
the hottest days in August you could "fry eggs on the
sidewalk" in front of The Herald Office and Norge Hus Cafe.
Did you know about their match-stick guns carved out of
spring-loaded wooden clothespins with the spring triggers
and rubber bands? For smoke trails you licked the match.

Mike was one of the Skunk River Boys known to skinny-dip
summers at "Stork's Hole"—or a mile or two north at the "5-Bs"
swimming beach (that blood-sucker-infested gathering place we
called "Boys' Beautiful Bare Butt Beach"). Whether Mike
smoked a cigarette from those we pilfered from Mom's purse
is one detail I don't remember, although he can probably tell you.

A more sensible swimming alternative was when we jumped in
uninvited with no enrollment at Riverside Bible Camp between
Story and Randall—participated without being members in leather-
working crafts, Indian beads and feathers and games we thought
were surely free for Story City boys and girls—some of the same

10/11 year olds who used a Benson mattress for indoor targets with .22s—while Mom was "Number Please?" at the telephone office.

Mike was with us summers when we stole wooden lids from the Hill's Buttertub Company—to use as shields for our Indian wars. Was it Mike, eventually, who identified the bows and arrows we coveted after spotting them in a small railroad shed south of the grain elevators? "They belonged to Vernon Farmer," he learned years later. It was future Mayor Mike who organized the stunt when several scholars, 1961, lifted Coach Clark's Volkswagen, and carried it onto the center of the Viking gym floor. Did Coach Clark ever learn Mike was key?

Today, Mayor Mike is so involved with Trees Forever that he can probably answer this question posed in high school science courses: "differentiate between the cadmium and the pericycle!" Today he's so involved with Trees he's accused of turning Story City into a tree farm, sometimes called Story City's "tree-hopper"—which in case you didn't already know is "any of numerous small leaping homopterous insects (family Membracidae) living on sap from branches and twigs". . .

I wonder, if for a wedding anniversary, he might drive Patsy to Nebraska City to visit the statue of the founder of Trees Forever, J. Sterling Morton (1832-1902). I'd better close this rough-draft poem NOW that we're approaching our allotted 60 minute time limit—otherwise The Mayor has threatened to have us arrested and taken to be locked up in that old Story City jail cell almost buried in the bowels of City Hall—so close to the basement pool table . . . Thanks Mayor Mike, we'll wrap it up!

(B)

MIKE & MIKE

(Nordeen and Jensen)

Summer. Small town. When two boys ditched their shared bike
to take a shortcut—from alley to broad Main Street's

old-fashioned bricks—through a vintage general store,
the generous Norwegian grocer enjoyed reciting these lines:

"Mike and Mike ride a bike. Take a banana if you'd like."
They chose the shortcut and banana every day until time

retired the kind man's daily rhyme . . . Then one Mike
unexpectedly peeled away after a car crash at 21

when two bumpers locked—racing to the races—
no time to say goodbye no time to study

that sudden learning curve . . . The other Mike
is now the popular mayor cruising along at seventy

enjoying lunch in a new cafe in the same remodeled
store with its original punched tin ceiling and

age-darkened floorboards. He digs his spoon
into a bowl of red jello with sliced bananas

that remind him of the Norwegian immigrant's rhyme:
"Mike and Mike ride a bike. Take a banana

if you'd like." Remembering two sets of footprints
crossing those wide historical boards, he glimpses

the missing Mike waving, fading, as the waitress

waits beside his table . . . Did she say something?

"Would you like anything else Mike?" He looks
up at her. "um . . . More time if you don't mind."

"Sure! Take all day if you want Mr. Mayor."
Smiling, she rushes off to help another customer.

But this Mike is not thinking about dessert.

(S)

POLICE USE TASER IN LOCAL POET'S ARREST

A Taser helped police take a local poet into custody on multiple warrants of possession of and intent to distribute poetry. Local police and state Patrol were serving multiple warrants on Barry Benson, 89, at his home at 888 8th Ave. Wednesday when Benson attempted to hide the fact he was in possession of poetry and resisted official commands, they say.

The Taser was deployed after Benson struggled with officers, according to a release from local police. Officers claimed cause for a K-9 prose-sniffing dog to search the home, finding poetry and "other somewhat sorted" unidentified materials, officials say. Benson was charged with possession of poetry, interference with official acts as well as intent to distribute.

He was helicoptered to mercy Medical Center for treatment before being taken to County Jail. When asked what the hell he was doing, Benson replied "Dude, I was just trying to sell my book of poems, and some undercover narc pinched me!" He added, "What the frickin' holy buckets is next, they gonna come and take my disc golf accoutrements too?"

Officials then added that they are also looking to apprehend Benson's brother, Steve, saying, "When we catch that elusive guy, we can put this poetry ring to bed for good. Once the Bensons are in custody we will have possibly the #1 and #2 most publicized local poets behind bars." Concluded Mayor Mike Jensen, "That's where those Benson brothers belong."

(B)

DANCING IN A GOLDEN TENT

(for cousins Elizabeth and Kathy)

One minute smiles and blades
flashing we ice-skated on
the Skunk River's hard lid

the next dizzy don't fall! minute
we danced in a breezy tent
to favorite rock & roll

the Twist Jitterbug Stroll
before you saw me I saw you
laughing with Mayor Mike

and my brother and your good
for everything husband at our
fun-for-everyone Scandinavian Days

in our hometown park during June's
bluest and greenest you ran smiling
straight to me after five decades held

their breath as we timed our first magic
kisses with an early Timex that took
a daily licking and kept on ticking

in the playhouse by your mom's garden
shaded by your father's funeral home
playing hide-and-seek between caskets

mysterious minutes later we were both
divorced then remarried with kids
dancing and talking in the beer tent

one minute we were bravely playing spin-
the-bottle with our cousin Kathy in
her bedroom we both loved her so

completely forever until no more
minutes remain all dancing in a golden rain
beyond every breath we never needed to explain.

(S)

BIG NEWS (FROM ROSENDALE)
THAT NEVER MADE THE FRONT PAGE

This might have happened in the Rosendale village vicinity, five miles west of Story City where early Norwegian settlers (some from homeland areas near Stavanger or Rosendahl) recreated a Norsk settlement with family names still so familiar to us today:

Boe, Duea, Dyvig, Frette, Gertsen, Haukoos, Henryson, Hoversten, Jacobson, Johnson, Larson, Lund, Olson, Omvig, Oppedal, Owenson, Peter, Peterson, Quam, Sansgaard, Satre, Skeid, Sunnoe, Teig, Tesdahl, Thompson, Thorson, Tungesvick (last to manage the Rosendale store).

So yes, that was the setting, maybe 40 or 50 years ago, when at least four individuals well known to us expressed the possibility of a craft or beings from another place who may have touched down temporarily near our Rosendale, Iowa settlement which remains today only in our memories.

First, from cousin Mildred Owenson Boe: "I heard an unusual explosion during a wild electrical storm, and figured it was a clap of thunder, or something getting hit by lightning. At daybreak we went out to check. The markings in the cornfield looked like a spacecraft had landed and burned its pattern with fire and all colors of chemicals underneath.

You could see where suction-cup shaped legs of the craft set down."
Then, from the Boe's neighbor, Marvin Kokemiller: "When I saw the markings and heard first-hand reports of sounds, bright flashes and colors in the cornfield I figured it could be some experimental top-secret weapon or aircraft of advanced design, maybe of ours."

From neighboring farmer, Miff Romsey: "This patch of ground looked like something big, very hot, had sat itself down in that cornfield."

Today, double cousin Elaine Olson quotes Mervyn Teig, who lived nearby this site for years, and said, "The corn was green, but it was burned in a cone shape.

Some say lightning, or maybe lightning striking a windmill. Anyway, it's a good story." Then he said, "People will believe what they want to believe."

(B)

FISHING THE SKUNK

"A metaphor is a bridge."   —Ted Kooser

Fish jump here at the chance to bite your bait!
Carp, catfish, bluegill, bullhead, bass . . .

Soon your shy bobber will dance
and your line will have a mind of its own.

Keep what you catch or toss it back,
so someone new can feel the struggle too.

We roped together a raft and fished from it,
but you can cast clear across this river.

The breeze spiraling around shade trees
cooled thousands of strong green recruits

standing in straight rows for inspection
while trying to salute with lazy wavy arms.

The fresh wind waving golden hair above their ears
touched the football field and baseball diamond

and the cozy golf course across the main road.
Above or below the dam is your first decision.

Above it you can let your limp line linger longer
in the cooler shadows of the famous Swinging Bridge

with steel cables looping through sturdy limestone
towers with 1936 chiseled into their WPA keystones.

Below the scooped pockets in the dam you can test your
talents for baiting and waiting from a shifting sandbar . . .

But you don't have to use a hook to love
fishing here. You don't need anything struggling

at the end of your line to make you feel you've caught
something worth fighting for. You can walk out

onto the wet dam and dip your hands into its secret
pockets. Every time you do this you will be surprised.

(S)

BENSON TERSELY TOES THE RUBBER

Turning 67 too too soon
I still dream of taking the mound
to the sound of bewildered fans
who spot my grand gray shuffle.

Then after their wonderment
at seeing my staid warm-ups
actually find my battery mate,
I face a besmeared lefty

whose smile fades slowly as
the curve I throw hooks almost
low at the corner and the man
in Wrigley blue shouts "Strike!"

CLAIMING A FIRST

Turning 69 too too soon I dream
of fading back in the pocket
to the sounds of befuddled fans
their wonderment at my fake pump
as the smile on the corner-back fades
while my flipped jump pass floats
to my wide-out receiver, and
the man in Soldier Field Stripes
signals, "Move those chains!"

(B)

MINUTE STEAK IN THE MITT

(for Ray and Stuart M. and Ken M.)

With every pitch I caught
blood launched from my mitt!

My battered palm's bruised
tormented target-pad throbbed

where each pitch not hit
smacked and smacked hard . . .

I flinched when our pitcher's fastball zipped
like a white meteorite into the round brown

moon of my scarred mitt. A teammate's
dad in the stands, a former catcher, knew

a rare cure; he drove to a grocery store
bought a raw minute steak and raced straight back.

Here," he said, handing me the thick hunk of meat
as I suffered in the dugout, "this should help.

Slip it between your palm and the mitt." It felt
better. We were winning... But the day got hotter.

Soon blood sprayed with every pitch I stopped.
The umpire, sweating in his own backwards cap, mask,

chest protector and shin guards, bending right
behind me to call balls and strikes, wiped fresh blood

from his face, sighed and said: "Hey catcher, aint'
that steak tenderized yet? It's pretty bloody back here."

A catcher's task is to call and trap what's pitched
while working the ump to widen the strike zone, blood

or no blood. So I tossed the tough steak to a stray
team of dogs who weren't exactly students of the game.

(S)

SOCCER SERENDIPITY

—to Kirsten

Field after field extends in placid mist
as director's wife paces chalk lines
on grassy dew-glisten toward glide-
hovering hawks as father lifts cooler,
blanket, snacks, first aid, whistle,
camera, orange Punky Ball from
Intrepid. Girls and moms will arrive
soon in vans. Field solemnity deafens
now without daughter calls for visor,
hair ties, I-pod, bottle, Band-Aid, brush,
"My Ball?" Sunscreen, sunglasses,
head-band, sweet spot, flip-flops—
searching: Kirsten, Caitlyn, Emily,
Bre, Paige, Kate, Katy, Kali, Lexi,
Lindsey, Jenny, Hannah, Krissy,
Tal, Karol, Jordan, Randy, Sophie,
Jillian, Caroline, Allanna, Clare—
as this noiseless patient web of goal
will in due time be drowned in sound.

(B)

SKIPPING CLASSES AND FOOTBALL PRACTICE
TO LISTEN TO POETRY IN THE COLLEGE LIBRARY

After running up steep stadium steps with the team
still wearing all our heavy armor after practice
I'd shower dress fast and rush to the library.

Pulling on headphones instead of my battle dented helmet,
I'd listen to those old scratchy Caedmon recordings
of poets reading: Yeats, Sandburg, Auden, Frost . . .

It got so necessary I'd cut classes and skip practice
to focus on the fundamentals of T. S. Eliot, Wallace
Stevens, Richard Wilbur, Allen Ginsberg, Marianne Moore . . .

Often I'd skip supper and feed my fine young body
chocolate milk, peanuts, pieces of cheese and saltines
in my dorm room. Spiraling metaphors blocked footballs.

My grades were thrown for a loss. Disciplined
tough poets coached me from poetry's sidelines.
Their famous voices on thick black records tackled me.

Dylan Thomas flashed mysterious signals
from Under Milk Wood that I often misunderstood,
but I loved their physical rhythms, the plunge and leap . . .

No crowds cheered as I dodged through that tangled heap.

(S)

POPEYE

> "But by the grace of God I yam wot I yam,
>   and His grace toward me has not been in vain."
>   —1 Corinthians 15:10

POP-AN-EYE por favor pursuing potentially pulsating
puissant passionate prancing pretties purposely pugnacious
pipe-puffer: "Ja tink I'm a cowboy?"—Rather a bilge rat.

OLIVE OYL—older than Popeye... brother Castor Oyl.
O-yez, our own orgy, OK? Flapper; measures 19-19-19 . . .
"So, ya like my tight bun and me clunky shoes?"

WIMPY—J. Wellington Wimpy . . .
Wondrous Wonderbread Wares When Windy Weather's
Wild: "I'll gladly pay Tuesday for a hamburger today!"

BLUTO / aka BRUTUS / Big/ "Well,blow me down!"
Bumbling bombastic boom!—boisterous brawling brute
by bulbous blind-eyed brow-beating bastion of brouhaha.

SWEE'PEA—the foundling babe . . .
Socialists suddenly scrambling stampeding serfs step-
stranded safekeeping so suddenly spinach-sailor served.

Or as I remember when we were boys singing:
"I's Popeye da saylor man, I lives in a garbage can,
and I luvs t'go swimmin' wit' bare-neckked wimmin'
o-yez, 'cause I's Popeye da saylor man—Toot Toot."

(B)

GOOD OF HIM

He enjoyed
pressing a pillow
over my face until
I couldn't breathe.
He wasn't mean,
just having fun.
He always lifted
the soft weapon
before I died,
which was good
of him. I paid
him back one night
while he was sleeping
by creeping into his
dark room clutching
a long throwing knife
and trying to look
like a crazed killer.
I hovered over his
dreaming growing body
until he woke screaming.
I laughed so hard
I cried. Boy was
that fun, for me,
until he slugged
my arm and I dropped
the knife and ran.
That's how it felt
to love and be loved
by a big brother
back then.

(S)

TO ANN, MY STUDENT OF WRITING AND MYTHOLOGY

There like Artemis
you run through
the early morning haze

a nymph
hair flowing
through prairie grasses

outrunning wind and rain
as my fingers of benediction
bless your noble forehead

my student Artemis
running still through
my ever-present drizzle

your teacher, Bacchus,
celibate with you
jogging through my memory

from years past
out this satyr's pen
dancing and drawing

across the page
into this poem . . .

(B)

TENACITY

—for Logan

A comical circus mouse in colorful clothes couldn't leave us alone.
The dapper little fellow followed us along the sidewalk as we left
a closed cafe—late at night after rain, shiny streets empty.

Of course we never meant to hurt it, not at first anyway.
We felt like generous giants, and yet this rude runt
aggressively scrambled squeaking over our shoes and cuffs.

Maybe it escaped from a traveling carnival and it was hungry.
Or it lost its instincts for surviving risky outdoor reality
after being spoiled by trainers' treats and kids with candy.

Gently at first, my son and I tried to brush away this pesky pest.
We tried running from it, but it seemed incredibly quick for such
laughably little legs. It reminded me of a boy I knew in school.

He was unpopular, skinny but wiry, one of the smallest students
in his class and the least liked. His true talent was tenacity.
He never quit in a fight. Even class bullies eventually learned

not to pick on this scrawny mouthy kid. You could bend his arms
or legs into pretzels, bruise his face until his eyes puffed shut,
bloody his nose, ears, mouth, then punch his stomach . . . And still

he scratched, kicked and bit. Snot, blood, tears and spit smeared
his face as he swore louder, screaming his defiance into the red
faces of embarrassed enemies who might outweigh him by 100 pounds.

My frustrated son knocked the brash beast off his shoe again.
It screeched and scrambled back up my son's leg as he begged me
to keep the crazy creature away from him. So I slapped that

ridiculous rodent into a gurgling gutter and yelled for my son
to run to our car parked in an alley. Amazingly, the monster
jumped at me from the gutter, so I hit it again, even harder,

careful not to kill it. It wouldn't quit! I couldn't believe it.
So I hit the little bastard much harder than I should have. Then
I ran to join my son in the calming cave of our comforting car.

After slamming and locking my door, I turned the solid key
as my relieved son thanked me. But as our good engine
roared awake, we were suddenly, powerfully, jerked backward!

(S)

SPAGHETT WHISTLING TO THOSE BIRDS

—to Hunziker / Craig/ Schmidt

Strutting western boots down streets in Ames
at times his six-guns nested in their holsters
hung off a multicolored beaded rawhide belt,
red rolls of cap gun ammo, silver-buckled

loosened Levis strapped low, peaked hat
tilted at an angle, jaunty patterned scarf, daily
so every person recognizes this saunter from
Frangos Family Restaurant culture cafe

with rumored after-hour gambling crowd—
not to mention fine Greek ethnic food
or entrees Italian served with shining silver
clattering white porcelain on linen cloth

all providing employment for Spaghett
to wash and dry and balance high each day
between his walks in leather along the range
from Maid-Rite on the East, wending on

to train-station (mall today) in western Ames
cater-corner from the theater he patronizes
while club-foot / thick-sole shoed, long-hair
brother Hamburg buses tables, sweeps,

swabs at Frangos beneath their upstairs
lodging symbolizing this brotherhood retreat
from epithets from those who do not know
Spaghett or city fathers of later glory days.

(B)

THE BIG CAN THEORY

"... like a melody you heard from the flowers when you were three
years old but forgot to tell anyone."   —Diane Frank
—for Chloe

Walking with my daughter she said:
"Jesus doesn't have to eat anymore."

"Is he on a new diet like Mommy?"
Her frown looked like her mother's.
So I quickly added: "Why doesn't he eat?"

She patiently explained. "Jesus puts stones in a big can
with rain and dirt and stirs it all up until it's yummy."

She looked at my face to see if I was getting it.
Apparently I wasn't. Before I could stop my tongue I heard
it say: "Then you must favor the Big Can Theory of Salvation."

She peered into the red throat of a yellow-tongued tulip.
"You think flowers don't talk Daddy, but they do."

She looked at me and I was in both of her eyes.
"What do they say Sweetheart?"
"They want you to dig up your Daddy's bones
and hold them and kiss them forever."

Needing time to shake the Etch-A-Sketch in my head
until it was smoothly gray again, I looked up at three
dark pines pointing to hazy rows of crisscrossing clouds.

When I was able to see only one daughter again,
I asked her what else flowers said.
"Every time they open their pretty mouths they say something.
Everybody knows that don't they Daddy?"

But I still wasn't convinced. "What happens if no one
is listening?" She smiled and squeezed my big mitt of a hand.

"They spill their words on the ground. Then the sun
sucks them up and they all fall down when it rains
so Jesus can scoop them into a tin can with some delicious dirt."

She dropped my hand and ran to an empty swing where I pushed her
gently at first, then faster and higher until she screamed.

(S)

PREMONITION

"I am moved by fancies that are curled
around these images." —T. S. Eliot

Forget the peach, the Universe,
do I dare to take a nap though
that's what I crave when the
premonition comes as now?

What if it is the last, never
verbalized? That restive heart
after a quick walk, heavy calves,
trick knees. Then whom to tell?

Four sons, stepson, daughter,
poet brother, writing group,
wife whose mother responded,
"How could he leave us now!"

when her husband, 65, checked
out so early? What would they, what
could they say? Norsk of course
are taught to clam up when hooked.

But again those tugging pains
in the jutting lower gut, like an
obtrusive marlin who swallows
the snare, dizzy before it's ever set

or those Puritans whose intestines
roped around a sapling, the men
from Iroquois lore spearheaded
into circling, bloody circles after

their own betrayal. Or our maternal
grandmother's dire directive before
dying at 64: "Don't let them take you
into any hospital, just leave me home.

"When our people go in there
they usually never come out alive."
Yes, telling could jinx forewarning
but with conscious reasons?

(B)

DISTANT THUNDER

rumbling through your belly
tells you not to worry;
the animal living in you
will, in time, devour you
too like like a wolf or an owl,
bones and all, even the foul
slippery ropes coiled inside
that tie you to this life.

Like those Native Americans
who tied intestines of Puritans
to young trees deep in the forest,
then forced the faithful at knife-point
in bloody circles until they stumbled
straight into Heaven with their albino God.

(S)

EPIPHANY OF MELANCHOLY WANDERERS

fall's matted leaves and grass
near garden spade and rake
hazed wafer skin of bulbs
placed as paint-curled trellis
leaning on creamy yellow walls
tangled morning glory runners
random angle-patterned laths
for climbing clematis vines
from north Canada to Mexico
interrupted now by bounding
beagle hounding her assurance
chords of life and flapping ears
yapping yipping steps for smells
under pastel sky of crested banks
toward clouds new-sprinkled traces
onto peat and mulch and loam,
as Lepidoptera ordered once
unplaited harness handling lines
releasing, now directed home
with canis sirius riff below

across my neighbor's fence
where monarchs migrate
late summer flutter
we dream of mountains
of Mexico windsurfing
of red, black, and orange
scaffold Danaus plexippus
hummingbird helicopters
sucking nectar from hibiscus,
near honeysuckle, hollyhock,
gliding toward beard tongue
from phosphorescent pathways
until a melancholy wanderer,
an editorial escort framed
to a sky-latticed fretwork
where a sovereign liege reigns
then every time a butterfly
appears like air-traffic control
resolutely venturing along
to battle tubular proboscis

and I had thought such beasts of air, field
and constellation oblivious to each other's species

(B)

28

A BIG GREEN RABBIT

—for Reid

named Sophie
was my son's best buddy.
She was invisible
to everyone except my son.
We set a place for Sophie
at every meal
with her own empty chair,
plate, glass, and silverware.
My son was four
when he informed me, "Nobody
can see Sophie Daddy,
but she still gets hungry."
They played together every day.
When I tucked them into bed,
told them a story, then kissed
them both goodnight,
I carefully pecked the air
where I guessed Sophie might be.
Every morning
I fixed them cereal,
juice and toast.
The day I moved away
to my own apartment
across town,
I left my son with his mother
who had agreed
to separate lives. I wonder,
now, over 30 years later,
if Sophie cried
as hard as my son did
when I hugged them
both goodbye.

(S)

RUSTY EQUIPMENT

Cattle circled a hillside water tank.
Curving clustered hooves kneaded velvet mud.

Cautiously we
carefully climbed
chosen hills,
closed ski slopes.

Slow green hopes.

Crusty equipment needed white glue. White
cloud cakes moved through blue.
Clover buzzed with breezy bees.
Cursive birds spelled sky words.

You carried a classic picnic basket.
I unfolded and smoothed open
our holey blanket high on the thigh
of that warm thrill
still so greenly new and you
pink above me, pink below me . . .

Glistening skin all over you, all over me.
Listening to windy pines on knees. One

curious cow
came close.

Mooed.

Glued, we barely moved.

Laughing lovingly you said:
"Great, now he'll tell the whole herd!"

That day had to end one way. Mossy. Shivery.

A blue string strayed through a curvy valley—

curling stream cupping steeples
cars passing pointing people horses walking
cold oceans shelving layered limestone legends . . .

(S)

ORANGE—YELLOW HUNTER'S MOON

Something in October winds send
ring-necked roosters to strut colors
as grain combines stir dusty gusts
and leave just enough harvest husk
hidden morsels for deer who glean
toward a creek as geese, mallards,
bucks evade metallic muzzles
behind milkweed pods, sunflowers,
mums, under Indian Summer skies—
migratory nighthawks, ospreys,
smells in the wind and crisp calls
of crows echo to roadside stands
farmers markets with brown sugar
apple pastries to eat with hands
along waves of roadside crimson-
berried jack-in-the-pulpit, cannas,
asters, columbines, gourds, against
that blue-gray autumn sky.

(B)

IN A HARD WIND

A pheasant sprints
across the highway
to a gravel road
then into a cornfield
ready to be picked
in yellow-ocher rows —
the bird's feathered head
wild as a teenager's
hair hurrying home.

(S)

A BLUE HERON

> "Nothing is trite along a river."
> —James Wright

stands on his sketchy
reflection in a river
where he secures
with S curves
living silver
from a country
band of rhythmic water.

(S)

ON A BIKE TREK BEFORE BREAKFAST

While frost covers trees
a gentle fog floats above
frozen Walnut Creek
along the Greenbelt Trail
near an oxbow bend
surrounded by lowland
timber, a downed looping
power line lying off
in a distance where a gusty
flight of geese not long
after a clear night of full
moon and familiar stars
Orion's Corona Borealis
startles a wild turkey
to flap off a tree roost
or a near-by mink to
scamper around logs,
to nose a path of mulchy
moss and disappear down
an ice-fishing hole post-
sunrise now as this
biker wheels a narrow
new macadam path in a
season easily overlooked
yet too active to ignore,
peers where a deer slept,
beyond for a red tail hawk
or bald eagle as the north
wind whips trees, raucous
crows, oscine ravens,
prairie grass stands when
biking friend Rico Carty

leans, divining, peals his
silver bell, waves, parallel
to Grey's Lake, pedals
with him now (having
seen a fox running in the
shadow of the red Union
Railroad Bridge) strong
toward a late breakfast
rendezvous at Summerset
Restaurant & Bar turnabout
just north of Banner Lakes.

(B)

MY HUFFY 3-SPEED

comfortably carried me
to a cold campsite
where gnats churned
over charred chunks
that once were trunks
of trees. A monarch
touched dust and faced east
opening and closing
church-window wings.
Bouncing off my wheel's
chrome rim, a rainbow
honored my young arm
with the universal emblem
of the spectrum.
My goal was simple:
don't spoil the spell...
But soon a male beard appeared
above a loud red sweater
tossing a stick and an eager
black Labrador retriever
into a wet mirror.
What could I do?
The spell was dispelled.
So I straddled my bike's
hard spine and pedaled home
to my first worried wife
who asked me where the hell
I'd been all morning.

"Riding my new Huffy Honey,"
I said, relying again
on my boyish grin
as I forced open
a cold milk carton
and sucked white
sweetness from its
mushy male mouth.

(S)

CAT SKETCH

She rules over a pharaoh-sized waterbed without baffles.
She never uses tools or jots stray thoughts on tablets.

She whisks her whiskers, swivels her antennae of pointed ears,
casually models a stylish fur coat without buttons or zippers.

When forced to reveal what she wants or how she feels,
she uses a variety of voices: lonely, happy, angry, hungry . . .

I surprised this secret artist dozing on my antique maple
desk in sunlight one idle afternoon with a clock clicking.

Creeping into the room like a critic, I clapped my hands
as she dove from the desk, scratching with her sharp claws

a rocket blasting off on the hard pad of scarred wood —
once a tree touching sky with thirsty roots digging blindly.

Breathing heavily, as if I was the one who jumped, I stared
at the cat's freshly etched sketch, my arms swinging slowly . . .

(S)

LAST GAS STATION BEFORE THE DESERT

— for Lynn

Squeezing the trigger, Tim shot rainbows into a Navajo's pickup
as Kim divorced her golden sandal from a depressed gas pedal.

Cutting the curving highway's hem, Kim parked by a robot pump
whose rubber arm poked a pistol's barrel into its metal ear.

God it was hot. Her dead Dad's Olds '88 smoked for a drink
while Kim watched the old Navajo sip spirits from a Ball jar.

He licked the glass rim, then he licked his cracked lips smiling
and nodding kindly at Kim, wrinkling the living map of his face.

In her white sundress Kim wiped sweat from her lip while Tim
palmed the desert-dweller's ten. Framed by Kim's open window

Tim asked, "Fill her up?" He looked down Kim's loose bodice.
"Do you have cold pop?" Tim nodded. "Sure. Check your oil?"

"Sure." Blinking at Tim's dangerously white picket fence teeth,
Kim slid out of her ticking Olds while Tim propped her hot hood.

He watched her glide through the dark station doorway where
she pulled a dripping glass rocket of Coke from a red machine.

She popped off the crimped cap and kissed the cold glass mouth.
The fizzing fuel burned down her thin throat when she swallowed.

The young mechanic joined her, rubbing his hands on a red rag.
Long ago the Navajo rattled slowly away on the hazy highway.

Tim rubbed his oil-stained hands as Kim stared into the desert
at captured cacti holding up prickly arms as if under arrest.
(S)

MEADOWLARK, GOLDFINCH, SPRING MUSICAL

"March forth!" directs Fr. Swope, my colleague
from the faculty lounge just prior to 1st hour drama.
"Break a leg!" I follow up after our annual pun
before St. Patrick's, Spring Break, and Musical.

March winds blow in sleeting rain and thunder,
melting crusted snow and iced-over driveways.
Color-splashed kites at 30 miles per hour
race into trees, power lines and tempers.

Dig to the bottom of some dead wet leaves
and find color crocus shoots. Pasqueflowers
portend daffodils, tulips, iris, magnolias.
Red-wings, robins, killdeer stake territory.

Geese and ducks dodge one more snowstorm,
thunder showers on frozen ground. Blue birds,
redwing blackbirds, purple martins return.
Wild turkey struts. Cock pheasant crows lustily.

Swallows, eagles along rivers and streams,
a standing blue heron. Fr. Swope sparkles
in tux and red carnation beside the Steinway.
"Keep the shovel handy—for lion or lamb."

(B)

THE FIRST FLY

Nearly the diameter of a quarter
he made a horsefly look tiny.
I like to think he hitched a ride
in one of those empty boxcars
booming and rattling over
the tracks only a block away.

Maybe he traveled from Kentucky,
Mississippi or Tennessee,
and I was the lucky Yankee
he chose to rest beside.
I nudged him with a finger
but he wouldn't even budge.

He completely ignored me!
A breathing mountain of a man,
I loomed over him as he carefully
cleaned his goggles with his two
front legs, while polishing his
wings with his two back legs.

That left him balanced on his two
middle legs. Must be handy having six!
After his spit bath, like a hairy acrobat
he walked on the lip of my mug of tea
as if performing for me. He was the first
fly I ever really felt like befriending.

He was good company on a chilly day
until he slowly taxied down the arm
of my lawn chair . . . Then he jumped
into the air, his body dipping
like a fat jet from a tilting deck,
fighting for height above the reaching waves.

(S)

NEW DAY EYES

> "When you change the way you look at things,
>   the things you look at change."
>   —Anonymous

Spongy soil under matted leaf and grass
mingle with spade, hoe, and rake, phased
wafer-thin-bulb onion skin pushed as
phrases profess tender roots of life.

Finger place of paint-bare off-white trellis
at faded red brick wall and mortised stone
right-angle-patterned shapes of maple laths
guide shadow rise and morning glory vine.

Neighbor's barking corgi-beagle bounds
yelped assurance over ferns and columbine
shooting silver cords down dank-dark soil
across plaited grass, lies in soiled hands.

Tracking steps, gaze lifts to outlined pastel sky
line-crested darkling banks of blazoned cloud
while tendrils trace through peat, mulch, loam.
Grounded soles track hazier new day eyes.

(B)

FISHING FOR PIGS

—for Heather

Two sisters
climb nailed
boards into their
grandfather's
sunlit hayloft
in a red barn.

They untie twine
from bales of
scratchy hay
then knot pieces
into a long
twine line.

They loop one
end and drop
the twine down
through a trap
door in the floor
to baby pigs.

From the pigs'
view something
maybe good to bite
and chew appears
through a hole at
the top of the world.

Run! Squeal! Push
brothers and sisters
aside like when
fat momma offers
her sweet spots
to nuzzle and suckle.

The sisters are
laughing so hard
they forget who
they are when
a piglet bites
and they pull!

(S)

BELLA

Fall's matted leaves and grass
near garden spade and rake,
hazed wafer skin of bulbs
placed as paint-curled trellis
leans on cream yellow walls of
tangled morning glory runners,
random angle-patterned laths
for climbing clematis vines
interrupted now by bounding
beagle hounding her assurant
chords of life and flapping ears,
yapping and yipping steps for smells
under pastel sky of crested banks
of clouds new-sprinkled traces
onto peat and mulch and loam,
unplaited harness-handling lines,
Bella, released, bounding home.

(B)

The

T wants to hold hands
with its close neighbor h
as if T needs to lift
the raised arm of h
to celebrate some corny
victory over the curvy
pigtail of e—all that
remains of the mud-loving
pig that tiptoed away.

STRAIGHT

through
a wire fence
this bold
blackbird
with a shiny
indigo neck
steps neatly
wings tucked
behind his back
eyes bright quick
head jabbing
left right
like a lawyer
trying to decide
wrong from right
with hunger
the only motive

(S)

FOUND POEM—in Response to an Editor's Query

It was just too much, too many images
of growing up summers on relatives' farms
permeate this poem (although my brother and I
considered ourselves to be city boys).

The ages of men, women, children, rutted
roads, Norwegian relatives pioneered near
the Rosendale General Store—most recently
run by the Tungesvick family, named after
ancestral Rosendahl, Norway homeland.

The farms are gone, as are those who worked
the land – the fifth and sixth generations
now live in cities many miles and states away.

Whitman's allusion reinforces nature's art,
paintings by Georgia O'Keeffe, Pola Lopez,
discussed with fellow Iowa writers Maureen
McCoy, Debra Marquart: "I lean and loafe
at my ease observing a spear of summer grass."

Stopping the car at an abandoned farmstead
was an event I verbally sketched in my mind's
files (knowing I'd someday write this poem)
after a job interview in a far county wayside.

I had to stop. Too much wind, sun, sky, wild
flowers, trees, brush, grass, warm sod between
contrasting hot sunlight, cold creek, cool shade,
I considered images of exploding whisp-seeds
of milkweed reeds, doll-flower-dress hollyhock
... but realized that would be in excess.

(B)

SUN

U
feels
the fire
between
the two
clenched
teeth
of N
and the
sinuous
S
ready
to bite
U.

A MYSTERY

Across the street a young woman
with bare hands rips out seams of grass.

She squats on scarred cement, a mystery
in the sunlight splashing on her shoulders.

She burns through the summer afternoon
like that pink rose behind her in the shade.

There's something eternal in the way she moves
without rising—tearing out green stitches . . .

(S)

UNWINDING IN A STUDY

> ". . . both the visible and the invisible,
>   the sacred and the profane."
>   —Nin Andrews

The ticking of the clock—in an otherwise quiet house
as I turn the page to Nin Andrews' "Notes for a Sermon
on the Mount"—reminds me I'm alone with my books

today without friends, family, finals, or the hubbub of
deadlines, lists appointments, conflicting conversation,
waiting for mail carrier, phone to ring, command of

demand for computer, wireless, e-mail, iPhone, stack
of 138 messages, junk mail to read or erase—algebraic
as the beat of attentive hours in the room, and you

notice your dog, the beagle, following with deliberation
each fifteen minute segment of dust-mote, beam of sun
shaft warming across the hardwood floor: a tapping,

a toil, a telling to me, to all of us, others who are gone,
separate, other states, awhile yet, forever, oldest member,
having just turned sixty-nine to this ticking of this clock.

(B)

SONNY

—for Harris Haukoos

Seized by the day
he fell under a harrow
and his mother
looking through their kitchen window
saw the way Sonny's tractor
turned circles by itself
in the field and found herself
outside with apron flying
racing down the long
curving wrinkled narrow lane
past the mute mailbox
across the loose gravel road
into the weedy ditch
then jumping the wire fence
never remembering killing the chugging
puffing brainless tractor's powerful engine
reaching her only son—still in his twenties
and engaged to marry the gentle neighbor girl
who lived only two farms to the north—
in time to hold him and smooth his dark
soft hair goodbye, his damaged head
marked for sacrifice by rich clean Iowa topsoil
until he closed his clear eyes
with his face resting in her lap once again
and a redwing blackbird on a fencepost calling
in the quiet sunny field as a mother's tears
dropped like the longed-for moisture
the crops so desperately needed
that hot dry year.

(S)

THOUGHTS DRIFT BACK

> 16 years as I witness my daughter
> proclaimed a Pershing Scholar
>   —to Kirsten

As cars speed hurriedly by our home, my daughter,
we sit with shadows on our glider and welcome
our latest accepted, published pieces, expectantly
sharing achievement with you, your art, your world.

We watch for someone passing to nod at you, to us
affirming our existence and accomplishments—as
child, father, writers, readers, senders, receivers
we await a recognizable form of communication

wondering whether our spoken, later written words
warrant reaction that can be separate, not quite sure
as Emily Dickinson seemed in Amherst with her poems
folded, placed in pewter cups and porcelain creamers

so carefully. We wonder or perhaps we know
when a significant unsolicited response surprises
in envelope, call, glad-hand-back-slap from someone
other than son or spouse or brother, sister, cousin.

Another car zooms by ("What color next?") or biker,
walker—waving toward us—responding to our waves
and I in mind with you congratulate them all for
their own contracted compensation with the world.

(B)

HERB 'S ROOM

When Herb was shot below the knee
by Ronnie Hunter, a teenager
(gangrene set in) target shooting
using a pistol with a bad firing pin
near the peace-making Skunk River
where squirrels, muskrats,
deer and rabbits roamed,
Herb's room was slowly moved
downstairs off the kitchen
where he painstakingly glued
model airplanes during that
throbbing yearning year waiting
for a new right leg to appear—
a smooth plastic model of a foot,
ankle, shin and calf that Herb
strapped on every day until
the rest of him was gone.

The lost leg itched as Herb built
balsa bombers, P-51 Mustangs, MIGS,
Hellcats, Zeros and Messerschmitts
in bursting blinding sunlight burning
flaming walls, chairs and floors
while screaming winds strafed snow
and sleet against the cold farmhouse
his parents rented on a high hill
surrounded by tilled frozen fields
where blizzards closed gravel roads
and the steep eroded lane clutched
stuck cars and trucks so well
that even bucking tractors lurched
through shifting gears and drifts
as Herb calmly constructed crafts
tied with strong strings to rafters
patrolled by silent spying spiders.

(S)

53

AUNT CLARA WRITES

(short version in *Antioch Review*, Summer 2010)

AUNT CLARA WRITES (1)

THE PLUMS WERE NOT SO HOT THIS YEAR
I PUT A BUSHEL OF APPLES IN COLD STORAGE
BAKED A BOWL FULL FOR DINNER
DID A LOT OF CANNING AS USUAL
HAD A LOT OF STRAWBERRIES
AND RASBERRIES
TOOK STEVE AND YOUR MOM
A JAR OF DILL PICKLES
HE SAID BOUGHT ONES
ARE NO GOOD

AUNT CLARA WRITES (2)

WE FINALLY HAVE NO SNOW TO DIG OUT TODAY
BUT FOG SO THICK WE CAN HARDLY SEE ROAD
THAT WAY YESTERDAY TOO
OUR CORN AND BEANS ARE ALL IN THE BINS
CHICKENS IN THE HEN HOUSE AND LAYING FINE
BUT PRICE IS ROTTEN
WE HALF TO BEEF ABOUT SOMETHING
WE BUTCHERED A HOG
SO WE HAVE SOME REAL GOOD HAM AND BACON

AUNT CLARA WRITES (3)

HOW TO GET THE BULGE OUT OF KNEES
IN YOUR WOOL NAVY BLUE UNIFORM?

YOU USE A DAMP CLOTH
LAY PANTS DOWN FOLD CREASE
LAY ON CLOTH AND PRESS WITH HOT IRON
BE VERY CAREFUL NOT TO SCORCH
WOOL BURNS EASY
DAMP CLOTH WILL SHRINK THE STRETCH OUT
HOW DO YOU LIKE THE NAVY?
WHEN ARE YOU COMING HOME FOR COLLEGE?

(B)

MY FATHER'S SILVER DOLLARS

When he finished the houses
he painted in small towns
where he lived, he loved
to take his speckled hammer
and sharp threepenny nails
up the ladder with silver
dollars in his khaki slacks.

Under the highest peaks
he nailed those proud coins
where the projecting roofs
saved them from bad weather.
It's how he signed his work.
Sun still strikes those proofs
of what he thought he was worth.

(S)

OUR DAD

—with influence from "Spoon River Anthology"

Postman Butch Clayberg told us about Dad and his dog
Bud, both sitting on a corner curb under a street sign.
Bud was dog-tired from chasing all the cars. Dad
turned to Bud and said, "You rest, I'll get this one."

County worker, Marv Braland told of the tallest steeple
in all of Story City—atop the Bethel Lutheran Church
that Dad was hired to paint in the '50s, providing his own
ladders to reach that highest point on the belfry tower.

Several years later when that church needed new paint
the newly-hired painter told the guys at the bar, "Do
you know what Ben did when he finished the job? He
nailed a silver dollar to the top of that tall church spire."

Rosendale farmer, Marvin Kokemiller tells about a $100
check Dad earned from painting a crib and part of a barn.
Mom pulled it out of his pocket when he brought it home,
took a bus to Des Moines to shop with her sister, Hazel.

"She bought a silver purse, a pair of silver heels. But
don't judge her for that says Marvin Kokemiller. She
probably thought your dad would spend most of it on
the guys by setting up the house at Johnson's Tavern."

Joe Bill Knous—who sometimes worked near dad
from Joe Bill's sheet metal trade—heard Dad sing
and recite lines of poetry from memory. Savored
stories and poems passed from father to sons.

B)

MY FATHER'S HAMMER

feels heavy in my hand—rusty, paint spattered, dense
headed, its smooth rubber-covered handle still warped
from his grip. This speckled handle resembles a Pollock
painting with complicated patterns of drips, lines, shapes,
and subtle colors of pale lavender-grays, greens . . .

Holes decorate the hard rubber grip. Some are filled
with paint, and others are still open in straight rows.
The scarred head has a blunt rounded nose
and two sloping claw-ears for removing nails.
I start to see it as a Walt Disney character, but I stop.

I want to look deeper, to see what Basho called,
"something like a hidden light glimmering there."
I want to stop talking about this damn hammer and try
to feel what it felt—try to be equally necessary
held tightly in my father's warm, strong, still living hand.

(S)

FATHER & SON & FOOTBALL:

To Mark, All-Metro D-Back at Dowling Catholic

Every fall, with Little League finished
we put on the cleats and get into football
in the backyard with my brothers and neighbor.

Dad plays too even though he's over 40.
He's coached us five years in "Y" and parochial.
He almost got kicked out of our game yesterday

when he heard director Marquardt advise the ref,
"Watch Benson's hand—call him for motion."
I'm in my 3-point, staring straight ahead.

Maybe I was swaying my arm or hand
waiting for the snap. Dad says it's cheap
to emphasize that call so early in the season.

"Damn, let's be fair!" Then Marquardt struts
his 6' 4" / 250 pound "I am a man " style over
toward us, and Dad looks ready to punch him.

Marquardt says, "One word and you're out of here!"
Dad paces to our huddle on the 45, red-faced,
looks at me, tells Standfel, "Call sweep right!"

"Mark, plant your knuckles 'til they're bleeding."
He could have called Theiler instead of me. But
we knew we could survive Marquardt's cheap call.

(B)

DAD

Heels touching
arms straight
down slim sides
pocket flaps
snapped belt
buckled good
shoes shined
tie tied
right
hat straight
uniform pressed
creased smart
buttons bright
collar in crisp
clean thumbs
like mine
mouth mine
nose and eyes
my brother's
your first I'm
your last you stand
at attention in
your twenties
behind you
a landscape
on photographer's
drop-cloth grays
browns whites
no beer or lit
cigarette yet
in your glider-
mechanic Sicily

stationed hands
no scars in your
smiling face
or divorce yet
no jobs lost
or lasting defeats
no sir still proudly
smiling waiting for
the camera's quick
attack 60 years ago.

(S)

FATHER, SON, & RUTH HARMON—
Walks to First Chair Oboe Practice

"Goodnight Mrs. Calabash—wherever you are."
—Jimmy Durante

SON:

"My first year here on campus after my tour of duty
to qualify for the G. I. Bill – after Yokosuka, Sasebo,
Tokyo, Hongkong, Pusan, Singapore. And I can't quit
pondering late winter nights, passionate young minds
delving into Oscar Wilde's plays, Hawthorne's motives—
hours inside coffee shops with friends and professors
discussing Greek lore over hot scones and cappucinos.

"And I wonder, did you ever have any relationships
with a literary woman? I suppose there would be ugly
spats of rivalry like Zelda and Scott, yet exhilaration
for contemporary poetry with lovers of the pen. Yet
I wonder if I'm looking to college for too much. Many
of my friends have dropped out, including Sarah from
high school. Did you meet a literary woman in college?"

FATHER:

"So, I'm remembering you, Ruth Harmon—my first
year of college, out of the Navy, Dr. Beatrice—his
"two top students," his quote. End of semester, walks
across campus to first chair oboe practice, details of
how you carve your reeds. Exploring wooded paths,
limestone cliffs. Finding agates, fossils. Evergreens
along the Cedar. Detailing emotions, losses, victories.

"But then my Navy savings were running out, G. I. Bill
not yet enacted. I transfer to Northern State College,
concerns with credits and lodging. I should have called,
met your parents in your white frame house adjacent
to campus. Now, so many lives we could have led. But
when it comes it's just this one. I tell my son our story.
I want to tell you, Ruth Harmon, wherever you are.

(B)

SHOOTING HOOPS WITH ADLAI

Some friends and I were shooting around with Adlai Stevenson
in our tiny town where we tried to coach his common touch.

During those sleepy games we helped him master magic moves
going one-on-one against a five star general who read Zane Grey

while hitched to a sweet old-fashioned cheerleader named Mamie
from Boone, Ioway. But why play basketball with a thin brainy

politician in scuffed wingtips , an ambassador to the U. N.
whose grainy grandfather served as vice president under

nearly forgotten McKinley? Awake, I'd much rather play
"horse" or "around the world" with Ike, who looked like

my alcoholic father, a sergeant in Eisenhower's regular Army,
honorably discharged with poker profits and a bleeding ulcer.

Dad fixed gliders in Sicily where he met Jackie Coogan,
the famously abused child actor, then a balding officer

no long legally linked to leggy Betty Grable who pinned him
up in divorce court (Jackie told a circle of laughing soldiers)

for loving pork and beans and passing gas in bed. At least
that's the story my uncle pushed the day I reached into a coffin

to feel what everyone said was still my Dad, though it wasn't.
It was the dull rubber of a deflated ball. All the bounce was gone.

(S)

SCIATIC LESSONS

(sciatica: (n) pain along nerve in lower back,
hips, buttocks, thigh, calf, foot . . .)

He inches across the new parking lot—
sciatic-hobbled at 59, this same sprinter
who anchored the Ankeny Relays 4 X 100
(one of the stories he still loves to tell)—
unable now to dodge approaching cars:

"Possibly caused by herniated disc, probably
not a tumor, clot, or cancer, reports Dr. Shirk,
who isn't sure, as the former 155 pounder
wondering what's become of Coach Winfrey 's
spinback —struggles to sidestep a shopping cart.

Was it from bending over graves, blurred dates,
names—listening later to voices from night cries
from codeine-dream terrors, tossing, vowing:
"Next tine I'll dive for those first-down markers!"
Says Dr. Shirk, "There's really nothing I can do."

"After 30 or childbirth," affirms his wife, "women
often experience this, it's not unusual." Dr. Shirk,
after mallet non-response from ankle, big toe, notes:
"Losing reaction from bottom of left leg up," and
prescribes: "Return in 7 to 10 days." Then adds,

"It usually takes about a month, then goes away."
How can this happen – it won't compute with that
70 yard TD around left sweep blocks from Olson, Bob
Moore, Jensen, Joe Bill, those not-so-many years ago.
His sons and daughter know these stories all too well.

(B)

TEACHING MY MOTHER HOW TO SMOKE

Needing to keep her nervous hands busy
my fidgety mother, a telephone operator,
asked me to show her how to properly light
and smoke a cigarette. In 7th grade I'd quit
smoking for sports, but I did demonstrate
the popular way to tweezer a tobacco cylinder
between her first two fingers and then take
a hit without choking during a coughing fit.

I also showed her how to let the lazy smoke eddy
from her nostrils like a bored actress in a movie.
She enjoyed performing that relaxed role since she
loved her "Soaps" on tv, and movie magazines she bought
at grocery stores and drugstores. Smoking helped her
feel elegant, confident, ready for a speaking part.

(S)

A ONE-POINT PERSPECTIVE

with emerald gold and rose shaded beams
of vibrant blue and gray over a purple
and white striped cotton canopy on
aluminum poles above an Army shovel
with dried mud clinging to stringy ash-dust
and a trumpeter standing on matted leaves
near a sodden green path from Mount Olive
Lutheran in Randall—with military rites
by American Legion Lafayette Post 59
of Story City sharply saluting this WWII vet
who served overseas in African and European
theaters as Army air corps glider mechanic
out of Sicily (captured only once by a Palermo
street artist in a wash of chalk sketch pastels).

(B)

CHANNELS

Mom knew all the gossip first.
If there was a fire siren
everyone called her
to find out
what was burning
or who was missing or hurt.
If a woman couldn't find
her lost children
or cheating husband
she'd call Mom . . .
After 30 years
and maybe millions
of requests for "Number Please,"
my mother was sick
of being polite
to customers on the phone.

She ended up pushing a walker
on wheels in an Alzheimer's wing,
mumbling to blank walls
in a new language
nobody understood . . .
One day she fell
and hit her head hard
on the floor and she knew
who she was again
for an hour or two,
asking the surprised nurse
where her sons were
and what year it was . . .

The nurse said it was like
an old television set
when the reception's lousy
so you give it a good thump
and the picture clears,
but it doesn't last long
and the screen goes snowy
again and you can't follow
the actors' words or actions
and every channel
looks and sounds the same.

(S)

COMPANION POEMS:

APPLE FOR THE TEACHER

(written on the last page of a blue book final exam in 1966
to English 101 Professor, Dr. Dwight C. Marsh)

after it. chase it
and hunt it down.
grab for it. feel it.
then watch it run

little man lost
know that others are.
run very fast
and run very far

after it—chase it
but don't fall down.
others who run it
are watching you now

(B)

EXTRA CREDIT POINTS

(written as response on the inside cover of the blue book final exam
by Dr. Dwight C. Marsh—with permission to print it here)

Some years from now,
When the grasp and clutch have wrecked it,
And the running stops,
Knowing where you are in time and space,
Gasping for breath,
And you guess no one cared enough to watch,
Look back at me
(Through black rimmed, ironic glasses)
And hear me say
That it was never there; always here and now.

(B)

A PIRATE'S PROFILE

You know you're retired
when a water stain
on the kitchen sink
looks exactly like
a pirate's profile.
I stand and study it
for a while—hearing
the wall-clock struggling,
icicles in the blue
window lengthening,
my breathing . . .

A pirate's profile
the kind I drew with a pencil
when I was in high school
to win a Draw-Me contest
for a partial commercial art
scholarship offered
on a matchbook cover,
which my late mother
proudly managed to pay for.
I stand here quietly crying,
staring at a water stain . . .

(S)

MEASURED EVIDENCE

00:30...1:23...2:22...2:34...3:33...3:45...4:44...4:56...5:55...
10:11...11:11...11:12...11:22...11:44...12:12...12:13...12:34...
towels folded at even lengths, 2 fingers from edge...cupboards
closed... one heaping scoop of pellets in dog dish, shot of hot
water stirred (spouse's age) to make gravy for eager beagle
who wolfs it outside (year round) then walks for exercise.

Hands washed twice to ABCs song or birthday ditty 8 times
a day (maybe 10) . . . Cords pulled for night shade windows . . .
(equal lengths) . . . Bed sheets even, none peaking free, pillow
fluffed . . . 6 Ts of ground beans for 12 cups of morning coffee as
he drinks any leftover from the previous day just for starters . . .
Cheerios or oatmeal with 11 frozen cherries, 3 Ts blueberries,

slight handful of raisins & dried cranberries, 9 good shakes of
cinnamon, 32 second blast in micro, half banana diced into
22 pieces, skim milk till all rises, stir 70 times or wife's YOB.
Dishes face front, stacked most-recently washed on bottom . . .
pantry aligned by entrees, food groups, all facing front . . . 11
brushstrokes w/paste for each tooth, front and back, then 11

scrapes everywhere on days needing a shave . . . 3 folded tissues
counted three times the time of day he sits . . . Later in the shower
200 scrubs of shampoo for starters, 6 soapy swaths w/cloth to
each part of body . . . 22 towel strokes everywhere . . . then try to
toss washcloth onto doorknob 7 feet away (3 points for a ringer) . . .
Closet hangers all face front . . . socks aligned heel and toe.

Slacks each matched with sweatshirts, Ts or collared shirts . . .
22 pens & pencils at right edge of kitchen table as well as in
basement study where sharpener stands at ready for yellow
Ticonderogas (the best that you can buy) . . . This had its start in
bootcamp (maybe a trait of family). "Busy days? OCD? Who?
Me?" says he. But this poem must not exceed a single page.

12:11. . .11:10. . .10:9. . .9:8. . .8:7. . .7:6. . .6:5. . .5:4. . .4:3. . .3:2. . .2:1. .
.

(B)

A FORMER BOWLER FINDS A MUDDY BIRD'S NEST WEDGED BEHIND A LIGHT ABOVE HIS FRONT DOOR AND TRIES TO DECIDE WHAT TO DO ABOUT IT WHILE STANDING ON A WOODEN CHAIR AIMING HIS EX-WIFE'S PINK MIRROR AT TWO BLUE EGGS

As he considered all the angles, or at least a few, he threw
looks at the frantic bird-mother striking leaves from a gutter.
She feared his mirror-shine reflecting above her team's two
sky blue balls rolled into a perfect pocket of grass, paper,
sticks, petals, weeds, plastic, string and wind pinned hair . . .

Then he remembered the chair under him—supporting him,
holding him up and helping him—was once a limber living limb
from a split tree that never went anywhere, perfectly content to
stay pinned to one spot and thrive there. So, stumped no more,
he knew he had to spare this messy nest to even the score.

(S)

A CLOSE CALL

Yesterday I found
myself in an accident
on Interstaate 80 east
of Des Moines on my
way to Mt. Vernon
to meet my cousin
Donna Jean from
Cedar Falls and her two
friends, Janet Tungesvick
and Suzanne Pinnell who
were visiting my brother
at Lincolnway Cafe
when suddenly
the car ahead swerved
to miss a hunk of truck
tire which hit the back
of my car and ripped
off the bumper cover
shield from end to end
and I may have been in
shock when two cars
stopped. They could
hardly get the piece
into the rear seat. I
turned around after
a time and drove home,
thinking, "I've lost my
"Veterans for Kerry"
faded bumper sticker.

(B)

OUT OF NOWHERE

My son's eye is a happy blue
staring at the TV over a pillow.

His voice during the next commercial:
"I'm hungry! I'm thirsty!"

Dimples frame his goofy grin, a big brown
homemade mole forever befriending his navel.

Next commercial he's calling from the bathroom:
"I'm ready for you-know-what!"

He yanks up his tiny shorts and says:
"Would you go daddy? I need my privacy."

Watching cartoons together, he says:
"Did that really hurt Scooby-Doo?"

"No Buckaroo, those are pictures on TV,
funny drawings that move, like we color on paper."

Then he lays me out flat on the floor:
"Do we have to leave our bodies here

when we die and go to Heaven?" Luckily
the commercial is over before I have to answer.

He forgets the question watching Scooby-Doo
chasing bad guys through a haunted mansion.

(S)

LAZ: A Found Curtailed Almost Sonnet

> "In any poet's poem the shape is half the meaning."
> —Louis MacNeice

Thanks, Dad, for card, cash and Navy hat!
Interesting birthday today, at school with Laz:
two long classes and 90-minute ethnic
studies committee meeting. Laz, four, started
making farting noises near the podium
while this woman was lecturing seriously.
I almost lost it. Laz was mostly great
which is more than I honestly expected—
a lot to ask of him. I hope to get
this sitter situation figured out. The one
I had in line was put on bed rest due
to complications with her pregnancy.
Not really worried about it though. It's been
just great hanging out this week with Laz.

Love—Josef Benson, Ph. D
Prof. Of English, U of W / Parkside

(B)

RHABDOMANCY

After peeling dark green skin
down to slippery yellow bone
we aimed Y-shaped hazel wands
at the thirsty jigsaw-puzzle ground.

Our sticks twitched as if tuned
(we felt) to a buried water channel.
Or did we only pretend to mix dreams
with unseen subterranean streams?

That same year another secret power
pulled our eager Ouija board pointer
over letters spelling answers, our hands
chasing the possessed planchette.

The plastic heart, with three felt feet
and a gold pin stuck through its one
clear round eye, moved over the board's
smooth hard skin like an automatic alien . . .

In the woods we found an open vein
where refreshing blood from the underworld
gushed like something sacred giving birth
into our tightly cupped welcoming palms.

We drank from that bubbling artesian spring, then
we jumped into a slow river peeling leeches later
from sun-pinked skin on safe green banks, nibbling
young field corn, smoking deadwood, napping, growing.

(S)

AT THE 1961 ANKENY RELAYS

—after arriving late in our yellow, 4-door 1950 Ford

"Rejoiceth as a strong man to run a race."   —Psalm 19:5

To Steve Schmidt, and Bill Smith who ignited our foursome.

The starter pistol smokes and
a tangle of runners unravels
as I crouch in silks almost
like a jockey till the cylinder
hits my hand and my teammate
recedes like a booster rocket while
my brother the anchor has shed
his skins and waves from the lane
we're in where arrival-departure
coincide or we lose a stride but
after scores of measured moves,
practiced blasts counting blind
exchange we're wildly tied and I
fly to reach him before out of range,
baton connecting fingers without
pause, I watch him snap the tape
under tiers of applause because
we've just run as fast as ever then
or now or for the rest of our lives.

(B)

PAUL'S OX

—for Paul Mousel

Before dawn, knifing fresh loaves of snow,
I floundered in my seven foot friend's
far-flung footprints.

Rising to the stars in his stocking cap
and huge rubber boots, Tall Paul stepped across
the necklace of our galaxy reflected in a black creek.

Yawning and shivering, I was Paul's dumb blue ox
plowing from trap to trap, breaking and
entering dark panes of ice.

We checked our chains for unlucky muskrats.
If one wasn't dead, Paul gently tapped its
wet head with a ball-peen hammer.

Then he saved it in a dirty yellow canvas bag
slung over my shoulder like a paperboy
delivering morning's offerings . . .

•

In Paul's basement I watched him peel
fur coats from slippery red muscular sacks
in the glare from two bare bulbs hung from hooks.

He stretched pelts over flat boards and pinned them
on lines to dry. He dropped shiny bodies into the trash
with strong hands while we discussed religion, war, philosophy . . .

Paul also worked third shift in a frozen bread factory,
where he stirred sticky dough like taffy in a giant
silver bowl with a paddle the size of an oar.

Working alone in his own yeasty room
I watched him row his way through
big blobs of dimpled dough . . .

After his floury fists punched and kneaded them,
punched and kneaded them, those living lumps
slowly, instinctively, began to grow.

(S)

RED-WINGS RETURN

Color splashed kites race
Toward trees, power lines
Meadow larks call farmers
Turkey vultures glide breezes
Goldfinches brighten feeder
Pasqueflowers harbinger
Crocus, tulips, magnolia, iris
Red-wings, robins, killdeer
Stake their territories
Canadian geese ride the "V"
Eagles toll their return
A standing blue heron
Mimics a bluebird box
A stand of daffodil below
Swallows riding the winds

(B)

THE SWEATER

—for Claudia

The boy gave her his old shapeless sweater.
She wore it every day until her father
envied the pleasure it gave her.

It thrilled her shoulders
when her arms pushed
through the boy's warm arms.

Her girl-back felt doubled under
his boy-back where they both were
collared by the same collar.

The sweater grew longer
whenever she cautiously washed it
then hung it up to drip drip drip . . .

She cradled it into the hot incubator
of the dryer to help it grow smaller . . .
It didn't fit her and it didn't matter.

It was the next best thing to being
inside him, to knowing him inside out.

It felt like a pelt—
fuzzy male fur
hugging her.

Her lonely mother felt
the scratchy baggy sweater's gravity
pulling on her only daughter's innocent orbit.

Each stretched stitch was a well-woven weightless wish.

(S)

WRITING CLASS PROTEGE

How long will we remember
eyes hands mouth nose ears

open feel taste smell hear
ourselves on this page

as the fire rages one ignites
the other feels the nobility

burning but also the embers
consumed by this creation

and how long will we remember
how much it matters . . .

(B)

DAMSELFLY

Finding a clear-winged dancer
on the fake-wood floor
I helped her onto my finger
and carried her through
our sliding door.

Her body was lighter
than a postage stamp—
a lovely letter Returned To
Sender into the damp
morning air.

(S)

17

—for Ben M.

I saw him decades later
in a scuffed linoleum diner.
He sat across from his heavy
knife-wielding wife—
brown gravy flooding her
mushy carrots, wrinkled peas,
meat and mashed potatoes.
His nimble fork and knife
danced across his platter
with rhythmical precision.

I approached their booth and cut in:
"Ben! I used to watch you on television
Saturday mornings on that weekly teen
dance program called '17.' Man, you were
the smoothest mover ever on that show."
He smiled at his wife, his voice low, slow:
"See? Honey? Maybe, now, you'll believe me."
But she was too busy chewing another
bite of steak exactly 17 times . . .
We all waited for her to swallow.

(S)

1950s COUNTRY & GOOD OL' ROCK AND ROLL

OFTEN AT THE TREAT SHOP—"See You Later, Alligator," when Bill Haley and the Comets brought "Rock Around the Clock" and "Shake, Rattle, and Roll" to The Story Theater. We danced in the aisles with Doris Jewell and Sandy Clayberg. Then, "At the Hop" with Danny and the Juniors, Chuck Berry's "Johnny B. Goode," Brenda Lee's "I'm Sorry." Jerry Lee Lewis' "Great Balls of Fire," Roy Orbison's "Only the Lonely," The Platters' "The Great Pretender," Ink Spots' "Whispering Grass," "Harbor Lights" by Sammy Kaye, Little Richard's "Tutti Frutti," The Everly Brothers' "Wake Up, Little Suzy," Connie Francis' "Lipstick on Your Collar," Fats Domino's "Blueberry Hill," Elvis Pesley's "Don't Be Cruel," Buddy Holly's "That'll be the Day" and "Peggy Sue," Gene Vincent's "Be-Bob-A-Lu-La." Santo & Johnny's "Sleepwalk," The Big Bopper's "Chantilly Lace, "Richie Valens' "LaBamba," The Crests' "Sixteen Candles."

AND A MILE OUT AT THE SALES BARN we learned Hank Williams' "Your Cheatin' Heart," the great Ol Possum No Show" George Jones' "He Stopped Loving Her Today," Tammy Wynette's "Stand by Your Man," June Carter & Johnny Cash in "Jackson," Les Paul & Mary Ford's "Vaya con Dios," Patti Page's "Tennessee Waltz," Carl Perkins' "Blue Suede Shoes," Jim Reeves' "He'll Have to Go" and "Four Walls," Eddy Arnold's "Cattle Call" and "Make the World Go Away," Conway Twitty's "It's Only Make Believe," Marty Robbins' "El Paso" and "White Sports Coat," Merle Haggard's "Muskogee," Webb Pierce's "In the Jailhouse Now," Vaughn Monroe's "Ghost Riders in the Sky," Patsy Cline's "Faded Love," "Walking After Midnight," and "Sweet Dreams."

EARLIER, MANY TIMES AT THE NORGE HUS (the former Cliff and Alice Sevold Cafe, operated by Mrs. Oscar Ritland and Mrs. Harvey Skeie) where relative Donna Nibe would provide fried egg sandwiches, Green Rivers, Chocolate Cokes while we listened to "Ain't That a Shame," The Crew Cuts' "Earth Angel" and "Sh-Boom, Sh-Boom," The Chordettes' "Mr. Sandman," Teresa Brewer's "Have You Ever Been Lonely" – while we played free pin-ball games all day lifting the machine's front legs onto our toes—yes, today's Mayor Mike, the other Mike, the Nordeen brothers, Frettes, Disbrows and the Olson-Hirdman-Benson no-dad-at-home adopted brothers . . . listening to Patsy Cline sing "Crazy"—yes, "Patsy," later to be The First Lady of Story City – and Marjorie Egenes maybe showing up when off duty from The Made-Rite shop (too small for a Juke Box) . . .

. . . but when the Tom and Terry Peterson brothers rode into town on stallions from the Sales Barn, looking like Elvis and Conway Twitty singing "Are You Lonesome Tonight" and "Hello, Darlin,"—what chance was there for us town boys with girls our age? But then late in the 1950s we pledged and vowed, "I sure hope we don't lose contact, man!

(B)

SOMEWHERE OVER THE ATLANTIC

Fish fish for fish down there
dangling light like lovely bait
while we cruise at 30,000 feet
in a silver jet, reading, napping,
nibbling cheese and crackers.

We talk and laugh over the steady ping
of nothing and the dangers of being
swallowed by much bigger creatures
with faces we've never seen up here
in the sweet-tasting whistling air.

Pale predators programmed for pressure
are propelled by constant hunger
in the cold absence of color
where sunlight never opens
its warm yellow door.

(S)

BUDDY HOLLY GHAZAL

Rage on, Buddy Holly, like either Dylan
or both against the dying of the light, rave on.

Catch the sun, wild man. Then that'll be the day
not to fade away. For the golden friends, rave on.

For light-footed boys and brooks too broad for leaping
rage on; and for us who are left, rave on.

One of these days as our midnight candle sways
to your music, your brightening glance—rave on

and then maybe baby, everyday, oh boy, well
all right, and for Peggy Sue down the line, rave on.

Oh yeah so early in the morning, calling friends
to run, laugh, yell—sing, it's so easy, rave on:

not to go gently, for us who are left and regretfully
for those not left, yes, for true love ways, rave on.

Ready Teddy, you, now, sing that it doesn't matter
Buddy Holly, any more any more any more . . .

(B)

MIDWESTERN STRETCHES—CROSSING IOWA BY CAR

—after Donald Justice

The tall corn rows
Have been holding their
Green arms out
A long time now
To kids
Who will not
Settle here
But pass with
Strange cravings
Eastward to
Where dark hours
Gather about a
Water cooler this
Is Iowa the
Mississippi curves here
Just before
The open eyes
Of a farmer's
Daughters plowing
In their bikinis.

(S)

MID-WINTER

Snow bunting on fencerow,
eagle nest web site, cold front,
geese over open water.

Vaulted clouds chill
a gem-clear quiet of pine,
nature's festival of trees.

Sole crunch crush of weight,
stillness from snowy tread,
newspaper toss, dog's bark,

muffled predawn glance
under a gleaming moon.

(B)

LATE WINTER

snow glitters outside curtain windows
through a door pane, a street light, a reflection
floating cold, smells that linger from a

wood-burning stove as early-arrived robins
flinch over loose-packed snow, dart from shrubs
then startle from expectations filling a grey sky

with honks from a low-flying V of geese,
and later along Walnut Creek a standing
blue heron lifts from its stilted shadows

from the thin ice along the shore line, slowly
flaps, wings, rides the winds into March.

(B)

FINDING A SPIRITUAL GUIDE IN A BAR OFF BOURBON

My mouth hung open like a baby bird's beak
as I watched the radiant bored stripper—teacher, leader,
excellent spiritual guide—make two lit cigarettes glow,
inhaling one with her usual mouth, and one with her other
slightly more private altruistic mouth way down south.

I saw the ends of both lucky cigarettes burn baby burn,
entertaining eager sweating stupid lonely pathetic men
like me. I'd hitchhiked in from Iowa you see,
keeping several states ahead of my diligent draftboard
feeling like a dartboard in the shape of Vietnam where two
of my teammates were legally murdered in the coined cause
called stopping the spreading of the disease called Communism.
I'd slept in a refrigerator box in a vacant lot for a week, sharing
the warm cardboard with a different casual cat nearly every night.

From his stool by the stage I watched a dimpled fool
with drool down to his third chin—dark baggage under
his wet weak eyes, striped tie askew, sharkskin suit rumpled—
as he threw a crumpled five at the nude smoking guru
who danced like Vishnu. With one of her six
gently waving arms she neatly snatched
the fin and palmed it out of view.

She kept dancing—more like shuffling her dirty Far
Eastern slippers across sand—with black outlined eyes
to the rhythms of a bored drummer almost passing out over
and over tapping sticks, gold plates and stretched skins in a corner . . .

Later, cherishing the French Quarter, another suffering guttersnipe,
I found the same fat fool stretched out like a burned out
salesman in his baggy sharkskin suit on a comfy curb.

He treasured a paper sack shaped like a bottle. Lifting glass
lips to his drippy carp-like lips, he suckled slowly,
then he kindly passed me the sack with its twisted neck.
I drank, then respectfully passed it back, politely observing
proper curbside late night alcoholic etiquette . . .

Until a street cleaning machine rounded a corner
with brushes rotating like surreal mustaches
steaming straight for our tiny public wake.

(S)

GOOD REJECTIONS

\# 1—A Found Poem:

POETRY—Founded in 1912 by Harriet Monroe

22 january 2003

Dear Mr. Benson,

Thanks for your interesting letter,
and for showing us your work.
I'm sorry it's takes so much longer
than usual for us to respond.
We'd not forgotten you.

I've now read the poems, with interest.
I like "Staid Coffee," but after reading and dithering,
I still find myself uncertain, and I have to say no,
good as these are. I wish I could be more receptive
and had time to go into detail.

I'm sorry to have kept you waiting so long.
We do appreciate your sending the work.
I hope the New Year finds you well.

Sincerely,
Joseph Parisi
Editor / *Poetry*

#2—A Found Poem:

Barry,
Thank you for sending us this work.
It may not have been the right fit for us right now,

but it was some of the most refreshingly original material
to come across my desk lately. We hope to see more
from you in the future.

      Editor, *The Missouri Review*

3—A Found Poem:

Your poems show a nice touch—
better than about 90 % of what I see.

      David Black, Poetry Editor, *ENGLISH JOURNAL*

TUNNEL OF TIN

"Close your eyes and let the waters take you home my friend."
—Morgan Freeman in "The Bucket List."

My first and last pet chameleon
explored the roomy pocket of my shirt
as I helped a nervous girlfriend
step into our little bobbing boat
that was shoved into the dark throat
of The Tunnel of Love by a grinning man
at Riverview Park—a small permanent
carnival now replaced by a mammoth mall.
Black water sliding under the cute crafts
bumping into each other and the tight wall
of corrugated metal, flowed through that hot
aqueduct carrying cuddling couples
kissing and giggling in deepest darkness . . .
You had to touch your eyes to see
if they were open. The air was heavy
and seemed, to me, hard to breathe . . .
A beloved blade of light finally
sliced open that tight blackness . . .
What the hell?! Shocking
blood stained my shirt
red and smeared my girlfriend's chin
red where she nuzzled it over my wet
red shoulder. Blood blurred our
red messy mouths and caught us
red-handed. The missing animal's
detached tail, somehow still eagerly
wiggled without a brain
in my sticky pocket.
I checked the boat, the water,

my girlfriend's hair and lap—everywhere!
But my first wild love was gone,
leaving only one blinking
red taillight turning
a corner.

(S)

YEOMAN'S REVEILLE

LST shipboard
in the North Pacific

papers slide / slither
files topple / scatter
cabinets bang / bend
chairs skid / slam
into bulkheads

(B)

SAN DIEGO DRYDOCK

Sitting on fantail hawser
gazing toward Coronado
Point Loma, North Island
red running lights over
lapping blue-gray currents

counting beads
on a short-timer's chain

(B)

DELIVERED INTO THE HANDS

—for Sharon and Bob Pollock

Where was Sharon's freckled father who tickled a ukulele?

Where were our two brother's who loved Dodgers, books, beer,
fried egg sandwiches, football, poetry, and the Navy's oceans?

Moth-glitter signaled from Sharon's dusky skin as she whispered
promises beside me in a messy nest of dust-bunnies on the floor.

Earlier our brothers delivered us into the hands of a gypsy
fortune-teller with jangly bracelets, a tilted turban
and hypnotic cleavage, who unfolded her flimsy card table
in the backyard to read the patterns in our palms under
tall palms, smog and hazy constellations of real stars . . .

"You both will embrace long lucky lives, but never together."
The gypsy and the scene looked carefully crafted on canvas.

Our brothers, shipmates on their small, gray, always wet
Outagamie Co. U.S.S. (LST) 1073, were finally honorably
leaving the Navy. To celebrate, they took me on a risky
bus ride to Tijuana before their discharge party in L.A.

In a Mexican bar a skinny girl worked our ripped booth.
Her small hand fluttered like a trapped bird in my lap.
Through a filthy window I watched the green head of a brave
little tree waving its leaves in coppery Aztec sunlight . . .

So focused was I on those dusty flickering leaves, that soon
I was watching my first and only movie in the trees—silent
scenes from the African Queen staring Bogart and Hepburn . . .

Thin tinkling tunes from a ukulele woke me. Several Dodgers
were at the party, but when I stirred next to shadowy Sharon
the Dodgers, the gypsy, our brothers, Mexico, The African Queen,
leeches, the German boat, brave Bogart, plucky Hepburn, the palms,
card table, bracelets, turban, smog and stars—all, all were gone.

(S)

0600 REVEILLE

—before becoming a DMACC colleague of Binh Dang,
   LST Executive Officer / Vietnamese Navy.

—To the SCHS class of 1961 Navy buddy system signees:
   Dave Disbrow, Joseph Holland, Mike Jensen,
   Steve Lybarger, Mike Nordeen, Bruce Swenson.

Aboard the U.S.S. Outagamie County (LST 1073)
during a four-month deployment in the North Pacific ship-
bound in his yeoman's office as stacks of papers slide,
slither, files topple, scatter, cabinets bang, bend, chairs
slam into bulkheads, dent the deck, flat-bottom sways
as he prepares X.O.'s ship mission "plan of the day."

Later, in-port, drydock due: blast, chip, hammer, sand,
weld, torch, cut, scrape, paint . . . ordered yells echo as
late evening he sits on coiled fantail hawsers to taste this
gaze toward Tijuana, Vallejo, North Island, Point Loma,
red sails in orange gold sunset . . . carrier signaling into port.
He decides on a ferry early tomorrow to Coronado Island.

Rippling ocean currents rock rip-rap welder-sparked keel
of LST Outagamie alongside wharf, fishing boat pier
as evening San Diego reflects in lapping blue-green waters.
If he were an artist he would stay here and paint all day.
An E-5 at 22 he counts short-timer chain beads, wonders
maybe a WESTPAC cruise instead of a Midwest college

hitch . . . to Del Mar, Oceanside, Long Beach, Arcata, "101"
bluffs, re-up for South China Sea, Souchong, Far East Sun?

(B)

OLD BLOOD IN OSLO

sirens me down from my balcony window.
Falsetto voices hail me from the empty
Rosenkrantz gate between my hotel
and the horseshoe harbor where ships
named for girls and buoys nod and ding
above lights burning into the cold fjord
so strong it carries cruise ships on its blue back.

(S)

HAVING AND HOLDING

—for Cathy Winter

Sometimes
in the night
a prehistoric stone
rolls onto its one blind eye
slowly hollowed out
by ancient hands.
It waits quietly
for a new life
to lift it,
to make it
sing again.

Sometimes
a prehistoric stone
is exactly what a living
hand needs to wrap
its warmth around
especially
when the stone
is smooth and round
and there are no other hands to hold.

(S)

THE SINKING OF THE EDMUND FITZGERALD

Overburdened with an unconscionable load of iron
in the 729 foot ore boat built in 1958 ("largest on
the lakes") sailing from Superior, bound for Detroit
that unusually warm 9 November 1975 day... then

encountered early next evening, a massive winter
storm near Caribou Island, overworked pumps and
radar disabled, unable to keep up with water in its
ballasts, the Fitz struck an uncharted line of rock

and listed in the center of an unexpected squall,
fought its futile battle against 80+ mph winds
whipping 35-foot walls of green water, then
without issuing a distress call, at 1915 hours

its shocked crew of 29, from Toledo, Ashland,
Ashtabula, Duluth, Iron River, Moquah, Superior,
Sturgeon Bay, St. Joseph, Washburn—all down
530 feet of icy water. None was ever recovered.

Now the haunting tale hovers through rogue wave,
fog-shrouded dreams of Lake Superior, more a sea
than a lake, with a mind of its own, so strong, so cold
where 350+ ships have plummeted with 6000 lives.

Legends blow deep—shipwrecks, snowstorms,
Alberta Clippers. Locals venture no farther than
where they still see land, a return of possibility.
We visit, go back, look, listen in awe to stories

of sailors, lakes, the sea—vast Lake Superior—
Bayfield, Whitefish Bay. Hear an old-timer say:
"God, I don't know. That sea is tremendous. Yes,
I'll go, but we're going to take a hell of a beating.

(B)

RUN DOWN BY A DUNE BUGGY ON FIRE ISLAND

"We lose our health in a love of color."
(Frank O-Hara 1926-1966)

Frank's funny nervy witty wordy jazz
riffs stopped that morning with dawn
painting his frozen eyes he didn't realize
the danger from a dumb dune buggy yes
it was July 24, 1966 and no one knows
now the name of the careless ass
who hit Frank because maybe his nose
was in a book of poems by Verlaine
or some Ghana poets or the Art News
puffing a Gauloise or a Picayune
thinking about de Kooning or Kline
or Pollock flinging sand in alcoholic haze
of sonar lights pinging close to fate's
beach-buggy forever framing Frank's
own "eternally fixed afternoons."

(S)

CRUISIN' DEAD ON

After the improvised graveside Steve Schmidt
military salute ceremony, he turned south on
Beach Avenue in the heart of Campus Town,
numbed by the finality, hardly aware of this new
highway, and lost in the reverie of images from
an abbreviated passing with no funeral mass
or sanctuary gathering, no family or obituary for
a man of such promise who died with nothing

after what had seemed endless possibilities . . . like
those words from editor Ann Frank Wake of River
Oak Review—"Thank you for sending us your
wonderful batch of poems... I obviously am taken
by them since I'm hoping that three are available
for us to print!". . . Not long after similar response
from editor Kathleen Wall, Wascana Review—
"We would be delighted to publish three of the

poems you submitted. Sometimes we say that we
hear a 'fresh voice' when we read poetry; I hear
three fresh voices here—a singular (or plural?)
accomplishment." Then two completely unforeseen
turns. First: "The English department of the University
of Regina has decided to discontinue publication of
Wascana Review . . . based on the Department's current
circumstances, which reflect what is happening in the

humanities and in faculties of arts across the country."
Second: "River Oak Review is closed. Lack of funds,
equipment, time, and personnel made it impossible
to keep the journal going. There will be no Issue 9."
Suddenly, after driving dazed for miles, Beach highway
drops ;down,immediately becomes, without a turn, a
muddied gravel road—like a lost lake car—drifting
slides, a sci-fi twilight zone of numbing denouement.

(B)

SHE WORKED PART-TIME TO HELP OUT

From September to June
her confused children
rode a bright yellow school bus
right by this gray pagan place
where tall rogue field corn
still volunteers from cracks
between sunken slabs
of oil-soaked cement.

The nearest town
is a forty mile commute.
You'd think some smart investor,
who didn't believe in wronged
spirits, would forget about the bad
luck that lingers here like a rotten odor,
and build a shiny new truck-stop
with T-shirts, bathrooms,
groceries and cheap souvenirs.

For years I stopped here
for gas, pop and candy
when I drove my young son
back to his remarried mother.
The friendly farmwife,
so casually murdered here
during a robbery, enjoyed
joking and laughing with us
about all the junk food
we bought—fluffing
my son's fine blond hair.

But now, when I look around
this desolate country corner,
she is nowhere. All that remains
are weeds and broken glass
and a rusty metal tank
that was dug up from underground
because that's the law now.
You can't leave those
gas tanks buried; they might
poison the groundwater.

(S)

VISITING UNCLE HARRY'S FARM

I remember the story Aunt Clara loved to tell
of that day . . . "we all drove to Kokemiller's for a luncheon
and by the time we got back a big sow with six piglets
broke down a farrowing stall's old wood fence and escaped
to the girls' front-yard orange plastic swimming pool!"

Our Norwegian traits were nourished on those farms
of hard-working Norsk relatives we visited from town:
"You can always tell a Norwegian. But you can't tell him much!"
—a bumper sticker said at "Living Word Bookstore" in Story.
But Uncle Harry always got up to do the chores.

I think of Uncle Harry even today when I listen to people
who say they never have the time to do what they love—
who'd "really just love to do it if I just had the time!"
Uncle Harry didn't wait, he'd always get up before dawn.
He taught me to get up every day and do the chores.

His wife Clara was a hard-working farm wife who helped
chore and raise their three girls: Shirley, Sharon and Sherry—
whose bedrooms upstairs in their old family farmhouse
were not heated in winter or air-conditioned in summer . . . How
they all laughed at the sow and her six piglets in the swimming pool !

(B)

AND SLOWLY PULLED

She rushed toward me
from the shadowy secrecy
of the hay-fragrant barn.

A whiskery head aimed
her skinny body at the skillet
of sloppy food scraps on the ground

where a wheel of cats smacked
and pushed like furry spokes
on Nature's hunger wagon.

The young mother's narrow hips
swayed strangely as she ran
to the quickly licked pan.

An unfinished kitten dangled
under this casual mother's tail
as she joined the meowing circle.

Knowing what I should do, I gingerly
gripped the limp legs of the unborn
who had no vote in any of this . . .

(S)

CLIMBING VINES

Spring spongy soil under matted leaf and grass
resisting giving in to spade and wrist in fog
over planted bulb thin onion skin pushed down
anticipating birth of tendril shoots of life

as tender fingers grasping trellis leaned against
a once red wall of brick and mortised crumbling stone
securely angled resting trellis anchor planted square
to guide the climbing rose or morning glory vines . . .

Ecclesiastes' sun also arising as Hemingway spoke
twice of each morning sunrise inviting eyes to turn
toward eternity as darkness overcome by cloud banks
launching gold and purple rays to greet a dawning day

and next-door neighbor's backyard terrier bounding
welcome reassuring you and reaching bulbs and vine
climbing, grasping silver cords from spongy living soil
beneath returning soles on solid grounded spirit

lifting your gaze upward eternally aware of outlined sky
ablaze over crested bank of darkened clouds overwhelmed
by suggesting life from tendrils reaching beneath spring soil
planted diligently with spade and your two hands and mine.

(B)

WE

howl brotherly
to every empty belly
as we lope along a ridge
above a river valley
where fresh deer forage.
We follow invisible trails
clearly marked by tasty animals.
It's cold but I'm not cold
inside my cozy homegrown coat.
We can run all day like this
without feeling tired or lazy,
slow or old. All those
running closely with me
know what we need and feel
without being teased or told
by taming some wild word.
We gargle a natural growl,
a high howl or quick yip
like a nip or yell, to tell
each other not to slip
on ice or loose stones.
We trust boundless belief
in our muscles and bones,
strong jaws, sharp teeth,
and our nuanced nose.

(S)

RULES FOR FRUSTRATED POETS:

Which We Sometimes Don't Follow

by Professor Josef Benson and Barry Benson,
for Kirsten and Laz , two of our
unique offspring.

"There are no rules."
—from *The Sounds of Poetry* by Robert Pinsky
(U. S. Poet Laureate, 1997-2000)

(1) Heed the image. Stack imagery. No poem without images.
Particulars.
(2) Use title to shed meaning. The title is the most important line of
the poem.
(3) Don't forget the referent. Metaphors are made up of the referent
or tenor,
(4) the thing or concept being described, and the vehicle (what the
referent
(5) is being compared to). Extended metaphors must include the
referent,

(4) Bring the speaker or persona into the poem—maybe at the end.
(5) Abstraction is the enemy. Avoid abstract in favor of concrete.
(6) Use complete sentences / punctuation or have good reasons not to.
(7) Don't construct every line as a sentence. Use enjambment
throughout.
(8) Free verse does not mean lack of form. Avoid very uneven lines.

(9)   Avoid chocolate bar poems—metaphor for solid dark rectangle.
(10 Write out of the poem, not in. Don't preconceive poem as idea.
(11) Arrive at the end of the poem in a place you didn't predict or
expect.
(12) Listen to your poem. Go where it wants to take you. Be surprised.
(13) If by chance you rhyme lines 1 & 3 and 4 & 5 follow the scheme.

(14) Create form where possible. Avoid rhyme, except internal rhyme.
(15) Avoid sing-songy rhythms as in nursery rhymes. Follow the pain.
(16) Welcome conflict and tension. Include motifs, create a pattern.
(17) Steal lines from other poems, other writing. Do not plagiarize.
(18) Revise. Your poem is not a house of cards. Prune one more draft.

(19) Keep every poem you write, letter you receive (including rejections).
(20) The sound of a poem is as important as the narrative or message.
(21) Study and learn to use sound devices, sense devices, word play.
(22) Avoid—ing words, adverbs, passive voice, unintended repetition.

(23) Yoda constructions avoid. Inversion of line shun and abhor.

(B)

LANGUAGES & ORANGES

By a blue
glazed bowl
full of apples
and oranges

you choose
polished words
each with a root
like this fruit

when it grows
in orchards
of languages
branching out.

(S)

OLD MAN RACING SPRING

As he leans toward
the finish
line

his cane
whips the wild
horse of the wind.

(S)

SIX-WORD STORY POEMS

Editor requests I try
Six-word stories.

Three years eligibility,
66 years old.

Got a puppy.
Losing sleep.
OMG.

Adept in the pocket
Dreaming. 67

My curve breaks.
Vision.
Turning 68.

At 69 dreaming
of completing passes.

Nearing 70.
Reverie
mastering the knuckler.

At 71
I'd rather
pitch MLB.

"We hope
you will
submit again.

(B)

PISSING BESIDE DONALD HALL

It was minutes before a Reading
downstairs in the Men's Room
not long after his young wife,
the praised poet, Jane Kenyon, bravely
died with depression and leukemia
slowly we stood there pissing
side by side at porcelain urinals...
If you're a man you know how
intimately private yet exposed
this public pissing is and I was
tempted to tell him how much I love
his poetry the Ox Cart Man still
one of my favorites and how sorry
I was about his wife dying wisely
talented and would he mind
signing his newest book of poems
I'd tucked wing-like under my elbow
while I stood there quietly aiming
my own pale yellow rainbow arc
into the universal porcelain bowl...

But for once I told my ego NO
just let this Famous American Poet
pee in peace shaking off his golden
drops too until we zipped up at
the same time and washed our
hands before a wide mirror
nodding at each other's
reflections carefully drying
our hands on torn paper towels
then he lead the way upstairs
to spontaneous applause

from a good crowd as
I returned to my seat proud
of him and my new secret
self content this once to
let what's loved gracefully go.

(S)

PAIRED POEMS

THAT COLDEST MONTH

swirled drifts and mounds
the studs, towing chains
school gym reverberations
on hardwood sheen, hoop
fans, coats and sweaters
shovel-cleared outdoor
frozen chain-link baskets

concrete court, stocking
caps, soggy mitts, gloves
SWISH of 2s and 3s
muffle King's approach
when Coach was King, hurt
hearing my flaunting curses
gripping grasp on my neck—

". . . and don't even think
about baseball this year."

(B)

DON KING / BASKETBALL

(Found Letter Poem 53 Years after Life Lessons Learned)

Thanks so much for the beautiful book of poems
and congratulations on having some of your work included.

I think a number of people learned some life lessons
on the outdoor court at Nevada.

In my five years there I was extremely fortunate to work
with many outstanding teen-age winners.

You were most definitely one of those. Thanks again.
Sincerely / Coach Don King

(B)

APPLE CAPSULE

My knife's
sharp gray
shark's fin
skims skin
like a tight
red robe cut
from a stemmed
globe's crisp
watery flesh—
Eve's juicy
eye candy—
cushioning five
mahogany seeds
tightly packed
packets
preserving
plans for Earth's
first sweet
forbidden fruit
stored in a star
shaped capsule
only visible
when you cut
the apple core
in half
and you see
it's designed
with prehistoric
plastic not
meant to rot
into the next
wet birth

until the slow
mushy death
of each ripe
pome's edible
gift branching
from the ancient
thorn guarded
rose family
tree.

(S)

MASAKI IIDA'S STICHOMYTHIA NARRATIVE, PART I (2003-2006)

Konnichiwa. I was so happy that you read my humor essay in class, and hearing your message. I was a little bit afraid of humor essay because of different culture things; maybe people unable to understand other culture concept of humor.

Thank you so much for your unstinted helping for me. I am wondering if you teach Comp II at the next spring semester. If so I would like to take your class. So. If you have enough time to take my general question, I will appreciate you.

Next classes would be my last semester at DMACC. After, I will go back to Japan for a while, and going to Minnesota State University Manketo. I do have to take 2 more classes for graduating DMACC. So, if you are possible, I ask you:

I would like to know about your other class, poetry writing. Do you think it would be hard for taking the class for foreigners (language barrier, syntax, different socio-culture perspective)? I will decide after your cooperation and I receive your opinions.

You ask how I learn about Des Moines, Iowa USA. Ryan Ingram gave me hope, an international exchange student from Central Campus, Des Moines, Iowa. He spent for one month at my school. We talk a lot of socio-cultural things. I found my hope. My jinsei.

DMACC is only one school that person from Yamanashi are treated as Iowans in-state tuition, really reasonable, isn't ? In Japan I help my parents run Japanese food lunchbox shop. "Hokka Hokka tei," a "to-go" shop like Iowa B-Bops; however , not hamburger shop.

My city is Enzan Koshu City, Yamanashi-ken, Japan. No sea, but mountains are surrounded. You may hear of Tokyo, Japan capital, it takes one hour and half from my town to Tokyo. There are funny and interesting traditional foods, mostly, I hate it though (hehehe).

You ask. Japanese suicide rates highest. Japanese Diet/government slowly think about it. Akirameru. Yomiuri newspaper, biggest and oldest in Japan,say suicide rates twice than U. S. And yes, Japanese doesn't separate to use both "R" and "L"—we never separate them.

About transmigration, most Japanese believe spirits could not die, and after people die, relatives visit person's house and tomb/grave once 2 years—1 year after he/she died, 3 year after, 5 year, 7 year . . . because in Buddhist lessons, even number leads to bad luck.

I have one 4 years elder brother, also 2 lovely dogs, chiwawa and minichuwa docs. My granpa and granma took care of me as child. P.S. I got big news. The Japanese person, Kamato Honda, who was recognized as longest living in world by the Guiness. She was 116.

You ask about Mt. Fuji. Yes, close, and most well-known mountain in Yamanashi. And about Japanese restaurants in Des Moines: best Fried Rice (chicken) is Thing Tao (close to Int'l. Airport), and for other foods, Shangri-La. Three Samurai (Iowa City) is best in Iowa.

Yes, I would be happy if you write long narrative poem about Iowa professor and student from Japan. Yes, you could use generic name such as Namakemono Koizumi (hehehe), or just use Masaki Iida. Fortunately, I was very happy Yuko told me to take your classes!

It will be distinct honor if you use some of my e-mails in your poem. I really like your classes—great information, fun, character—your classes were the best at DMACC for me. Maybe you work too hard. Grandpa tells me, "Do not work more or less than your income."

Soon I complete B. S. degree majoring Psych, minor Sociology, will return to Japan, maybe train students learning English. And you join my business? J Yorokobi. Thank you for all your responses, with your kindness. I really appreciate you. Oyasuminasai.

Yours sincerely,
Namakemono Koizumi aka Masaki Iida

(B)

RIVER HORSE

Slowly
hugely, in-
credibly ponder-
ously a hippopotamus
lumbers up a ramp from
his private buoyant pool
in the free St. Louis zoo,
where I choose to belong to
a gawking group of two-legged
creatures with cameras clicking,
standing around joking, pointing,
laughing at the small-eared, big-
mouthed, stump-toothed, four-toed
herbivorous river horse who harbors
natural anger and shockingly kills
more people in the wild each year
than all the alligators and quick
cranky crocodiles put together . . .
Cunningly surprising us on his
side of the metal fence, this
obese yawning comedian turns
his backside toward us and
twirls a tiny tail like
a cute propeller that
becomes a perfect
manure spreader
scattering
people.

(S)

VIETGURL'S FOUND POETRY

"How much pleasure they lose . . .
who take away the liberty of a poet,
and fetter his feet in the shackles of a historian."
—Samuel Taylor Coleridge (1772-1834)

Minh Phan to her community college creative writing teacher:

"I had a lot of fun in your class. Great teacher. Keep it up! I hope I can help you here. My two essays and research paper. And Vietnamese vocabulary and history you ask me. If you have other questions for your story-poem let me know. I want to be one of first to read it!"

AO-DAI—Blouse? Dress? The one I brought for teaching the class traditional Vietnamese dress worn by women. 1945-1946: Democratic Republic of N. Vietnam: Ho Chi Minh president, 1954-1969 ("George Washington of his country"). U. S. Pressident Truman (1945-1953).

BA-MUOI-BA—Alcoholic drink like a beer? Famous in bars in the war. 1954-1955: Dien Bien Phu cease fire/Vietminh defeat French Republic of S. Vietnam (Ngo Dinh Diem). U. S. President Eisenhower (1953-1961).
'59-'60s G. I.s: "The daytime is ours, but the night belongs to Charlie."

BIEN-HOA—Town with a French Provincial Hospital. River there: Dong Nai River / Xong Dong Nai. 1960-1963: Viet Cong. Buddhist crisis (Diem). U. S. President Kennedy (1961-1963) ; JFK assassination. 1964: Lyndon B. Johnson soundly defeats Senator Barry Goldwater.

COM BE TET—Brown fried rice? 1966: U. S. bombs Haiphong and Hanoi. 1968: Hubert H. Humphrey defeated by Nixon. U. S. President Johnson 91963-1969): Policy of "Rolling Thunder," Tonkin GulfResolution, Marines to Da Nang; LBJ: "Light at the end of the tunnel."

DIEN CAI DAU—"Stupid and crazy in the head." 1967: Nguyen Van Thieu elected President of South Vietnam. 1968-1969: Tet Offensive 1968: MLK, RFK assassinated. Walter Cronkite predicts the war cannot be won. Chicago riots. 1969: Ho Chi Minh dies at 79. President Nixon (1969-1974). 1971: Lt. Calley found guilty of murder at My Lai massacre.

EM YEU EM—I love you. ANH YEU EM – Boyfriend to girlfriend. EM YEU ANH—Girlfriend says to boyfriend. 1970-1971: Kent State / National Guard shootings. Cambodian Incursion. Laotian invasion. 200,000 anti-war demonstrators in NYC. 1972: U. S. bombs Hanoi again.

MPSs / PIASTERS—Military currency. Vietnamese money or U. S. ? I don't know? TET: Vietnam Lunar New Year holiday season. Vietminh: VN communist forces fighting French before 1954. 1972: Easter Offensive.
Watergate. Nixon landslide over peace candidate George McGovern.

NUOC-MAM—Flavoring spice or fish sauce used most in Vietnam. 1973-1974: Cease fire / POWs return. Nixon resignation. 1974: President Ford (1974-1977) offers clemency to draft evaders and military deserters;
Pol Pot's K mer Rouge terror in Cambodia and crossing into Vietnam.

XICH-LO—Ricksha-cab, bicycle in back pulls a person in carrier in front (two big wheels) where passenger sits. 1975: Fall of Saigon. U. S. President Ford (1974-1977). War ends in 1975. 1977: Iowa gov. Robert Ray opens Iowa borders to "boat people" immigrants (Vietnam, Laos, Cambodia).

Update . . . from a PBS television program, "History Detectives"—in Hanoi, an exchange of Vu Dinh Doan / North Vietnamese soldier's captured red 1966 wartime diary, for a bundle of letters, written by Robert Frazure, an American soldier, that had been kept in Vietnam.

The war (1954-1975), as reported in "History Detectives," resulted in deaths of estimated three million Vietnamese, and 58,000 U. S. soldiers. The U. S. and Vietnam normalized relations in 1995. U. S. President Bill Clinton (1993- 2001).

You ask about meaning of Vietnamese names in our class. Nha Trang together can be a name of a city or separately can be two names for a girl / woman. Other than my name, I don't know what else is the meaning of—

Minh Phan

(B)

FEEDING THE QUEEN

After spraying ant poison along windowsills,
then placing white plastic igloos of lethal crystals
in the air vent in the floor of our spare room
so, as the box ensures, workers would carry them
to the heart of the colony and feed them to their queen,
I clicked off the light and closed the hollow door.

When I entered the room the next morning, on the floor
lay dead and dying members of a slave-based monarchy.
They might have been a scouting party, maybe thirty.
I pinched the suffering ones out of their tiny misery.
Then I saw one lifting the head of a slain companion.
The head only... as if Hamlet had six legs and antennae.

(S)

THE LAST GUEST

dipped through a dark doorway
and hovered between two open
windows without screens.
Cradling its soft head in my hands
I helped deliver its stringy body
into a cold canal of wind. It
hurried over the black pyramid
of my neighbor's roof – shrinking,
eagerly it seemed to me – toward
a blinking switchboard of stars.

(S)

VILLA NELLE CEMETERY PLOT HOMONYMS:
A MAGAZINE FOUND IN EVERY RIFLE

—to Jon Olson, Bob Heise, Mike Jensen (who were there)

An array of batteries to sell to track spring's
fantasy of unsheared scaled bearded miners
in ice caves of winter's artesian springs—

coal mine cells, cavern corridors sprung
by writers whose pubs were mostly minor
arrayed with battery vault charges sprung

from .22s targeted towards mattress springs
charged with admission for drafting minors
from winter caverns of artesian spring

to baseball battery taut coiled to spring
though not to assault, as an under-miner
with an array of batteries following spring's

coal-battered major key scale rising to spring
in tempered law degrees for scales minors'
channel chambers of winter's artesian springs

teamed for small town custody sprung
softball leagues strung in double minors
played as battery tube mates tracking spring's
double-dammed Skunk River by artesian springs.

(B)

POEM TO BE READ AT 3 P. M.

—after Donald Justice

Including the diner
On the outskirts
The town of Nevada
At 3 pm
Was bright but
For my dark booth
And at the counter
My old football coach
Gripped a chipped mug
I should have said
Hello but who knew
He'd go home
Jot a note to his family
At forty
Then shoot himself
This poem
Is for him who
Turned his light off

(S)

MARGINAL COMMENTS

    —a two-year odyssey

We like your haiku style
but think connecting the images
weakens them. I'd like to see
one or two of three of them
as separate entries. Let me
know what you think

      •

We liked "Fall squirrel"
but wondered if
it might be tightened up.
Think about it.
Sorry. None of these others
seem quite right.

      •

You might think—
if you haven't done so already
and rejected the idea—
of distancing "Conclusion"
and putting it into
third person.

      •

Still more comment
about "Conclusion"—
think on it
if I haven't tried
your patience
too much already.

      •

Think as well
about focusing on the
dialog. Attributions
don't really seem
necessary – or
am I misreading?

                    •

I've underlined (forgive me)
parts that seem to me
to be crucial
to your idea.
Let me know
what you think.

                    •

Still more quibbling / fiddling!
I've underlined and numbered
the lines that seem (to me)
to make the poem
(but it may not be the poem
you have in mind).

                    •

Ahh me! Still sorry—
but, in some recompense,
here are the last two Reviews
for you to lick your wounds over.
If you give up on me
I will understand.

                    •

"Staid Coffee" is interesting but
seems a bit wordy. Think about
focusing mostly on the voices—
the parts that seem (to me) to be
your essential poem.
Think on it.

•

We like "song of Solomon"
although we feel the narrative
and expository pace are arbitrarily
imposed upon the form (or vice versa);
your stanzas don't help in finding
a rhythm to help to tell the story.

•

We'd like to publish
your revised "Staid Coffee"
in our Winter issue. Please
check the enclosed page proof,
make any necessary corrections,
and return with your response.

•

When we receive this
signed letter back from you
we will send a check and give you
or your public library or a relative
or friend a complimentary
one-year subscription.

(B)

GLIDING

The final time
I phoned my father
he was already a glider.

The sober neighbor
who found him,
stretched out on the floor

of his bathroom,
guessed my Dad died
about an hour before I called.

A sergeant in the Army
Dad fixed gliders in Sicily
during the Second World War.

Now his arms were wings
of a quiet glider
without an engine.

His curved body
on the curving horizon,
air flowing over

but not through him, flying
alone without direction,
fuel, or communication . . .

(S)

AN ELEGY TO DORIS

> ". . . goddess of the sea, daughter of the Titan, Oceanus,
> wife of Nereus ("the Old Man of the Sea") mother
> of Oceanids, fifty lovely Nereids of the sea . . ."

And with iambic pentameter I'll try to make this poem classy
though most of us know, Doris, you could tend to be sassy.

The time up the apple tree your sister thought we were mad at her
and said, "Doris, neither one of you two will ever be a pastor."

Years later you claimed, "I made an ass of myself at our reunion."
I countered, "That wasn't a setting for sharing communion."

You replied, "Hey you! We're crazy!" I said, "Thanks, Doris Jewell,
You stuck up for siblings, and our dads—and you were nobody's fool."

When Mrs. Wallace Wicks said I should be in a pulpit reading scripture
you said, "There's something just very radically wrong with that picture."

Maybe because years before when four of us were playing Truth or Dare
you just gave out dares—with Sandy and Margie each being there.

You claimed you cheerleaders back then "just weren't good at sports,"
but you all were such good friends according to most honest reports.

Years later when both of us had been married and divorced, you'd visit
from Santa Cruz, and we'd arrange to have coffee. And we enjoyed it –

sharing memory and conversation, maybe meeting at Valhalla for lunch
or perhaps, years later, from San Jose to Royal fork to share brunch.

Sister Anna said: "Doris felt there was a special friendship between you two.
Every time she was going back to Story she was excited to be seeing you."

And now, Doris, though so many of us are so sad you have passed,
with this roundabout elegy I hope these memories of you will last.

(B)

GASPING ON THE BEACH OF CHANCE

On a double Ferris Wheel in the rain,
above people pulsing through the midway
like the bright veins of an electric beast,
I saw the Fair—my head scraping clouds.

Brought back to earth—my stomach
climbing my throat, and my knuckles white—
I floated past talking tents.
Men with blueprints on their arms

were casting temptations at my shining face,
trying to seine, with a net of words, all
the slippery quarters in my dark pockets,
and leave me gasping on the beach of chance.

Clutching a plaster idol, I tried to swim
upstream against a current of people
in a flood of music, lights and screams,
lost like a sleeper in one of his dreams.

(S)

GRASS, TREES, SKY, RIVERBANK

Pass a day-old ashen fireplace
and birds are the only sound
until a fish jumps near Skunk River's bank
with wildflox coloring the ground.

June breezes remember your skin
while a meadowlark out-trills a crow
and you divorce yourself from cares
releasing tensions spirits flow

like a teenager barefoot on winding paths
your youthful soul absorbs the sun
with buds and branches swaying in wind
you feel forest and you are one

with grass, trees, sky and riverbank
reflecting greens below and blues above
as you think of bullheads or smoking-wood
with Story City friends in these woods you love.

(B)

KATHY

We climbed above
tears and bruises
into the rough arms
of old elms
to sit in their green
swaying rooms kissing
through long afternoons
listening to grasshoppers
crackle in the sharp
dry weeds below . . .

(S)

A NAP IN SHAKESPEARE'S CAP

Crisp legions clashed in streets

when she crawled in with me
under a mothering pine and a rug
on loan from a clothesline.

We met in a doorway where cold
wind knifed our thin coats
and clouds canceled
constellations.

She idled on my chest
as our whiskers mixed.

We slept . . .

She was the kind that napped
in Shakespeare's foolscap,
licked a boar's dripping fat
from the gold plate
of Alexander The Great,

curled in Cleopatra's lovely lap,
licking her own worshiped fur
while the queen's boats hissed

and the smiling asp kindly kissed . . .

We purred good words
shivering at dawn,

Then moved on.

(S)

"ONE SANDWICH ONLY"

(– at Phil Peterson's funeral)

"Vart livs tid, den er sytti ar og, nar der er megen styrke, atti ar, og
dets herlighet et moie og tomhet; for hastig blev vi drevet fremad,
og vi floi avsted."
    —SALMENES 90:10

Traveling back to my Roland-Story home town for
a funeral for Phil Peterson, high school hero, passed
at 77 following a 10-day illness. Taps echo 3-note riffs
as part of the Presentation of the Flag for two years

military service in Germany after All-State honors
in high school basketball, football, MVP recognition
at Waldorf College, followed by a 38-year career
as truck driver and hog buyer for Farmland Foods.

Standing in line for the church basement brunch
I recognize middle school teammates Tom Peterson
(and his 7' 1" son), and Joe Bill Knous & Kathy. We
all recall the now-razed Peterson horse ranch . . .

when my 86-year-old 2nd cousin Lorraine frantically
waves me to her table; when conversation seems to halt,
the woman beside her, Solvay Stole Twedt, says to me,
"I was your teacher." I look, pause, and have to say:

"You don't look old enough to be my teacher." She takes
my hand, recalling, squeezes. I continue, "Didn't you ask
me to stay after class and sing, "Beautiful brown eyes, I'll
never love blue eyes again . . ."? "No," she says as her

husband turns. I quickly reply, "Maybe it was Barbara
Jacobson Doolittle, or Ramona Erickson?" Solvay says,
"Barbara died this last year." We pause, for Barbara's
passing, for lost friends, relatives, classmates, stories.

Later, across the room, as I look through photos for
our Confirmation Class (now 55 years past), I notice
Esther Wicks approaching. She asks, "Do you remember
our Immanuel Lutheran Sunday school class?"

"Yes," I stumble, "you said you'd never be satisfied
until you saw me in the pulpit." Esther smiles, and replies,
"Yes, and, of course, when our good friend, Doris Jewell heard
about that she said, "I have a hard time with that picture."

Cousin Kenny Frette approaches, remarks on the turnout,
reads the note near the food trays: ONE SANDWICH ONLY.
We all agree, "Phil would have laughed at that." I add, "He
always had good stories to tell us, every time we saw him."

Much later, physically alone in the narthex, the nave,
I walk down the aisle, step into the high, imposing
pulpit and read, to those rows of unseen souls and spirits,
the first draft for this poem and prayer for Phil Peterson.

(B)

A GOOD CREMATION

"It was a good cremation,"
my uncle said
even though his friend
was dead.

"They put his ashes
into a little jar.
It's surprising when burned
how small we are."

(S)

NORWEGIAN FUNERAL

Our dead are parked in the lobby
when we sign the fancy guest book.
Heavy women with canes who can't climb
stairs ride a quiet machine up a wall.

We sit where we're told to sit
by amateur ushers who mean well.
We might find ourselves by a woman
with small bones fidgeting on a rubber ring.

Or a skeletal neighbor might be wearing his
wrinkled shirt inside out, one green
sock and one brown. We're trained
from birth not to point this out.

Roped pews up front are reserved for family
and next of kin—best seats in the house.
We nod under the mumbled spell of the Bible,
then crucify several songs from a ragged hymnal.

Drowsy after the service, we steer
powerful machinery to a small cemetery
where tents are pitched as if for a picnic,
a party or a traveling circus. Here we feel

closer to the dead and even to each other,
watching a pastor with nothing on his head
scatter soil over a copper-colored coffin.
Good clean dirt clings to our best shoes.

We hug and cry and stumble
on the turned turf. We walk slowly—

one does not run—back to our waxed cars
reflecting in the sun. We return to the church

where women fix a meal in the basement:
egg salad sandwiches, kringla, apple cider,
coffee. We collect around long brown tables
eating, drinking and embroidering our history.

(S)

CRITICAL PRAISE: A Found Poem

Many thanks for sending your poems
our way again, and I did want to
congratulate you on your well-deserved fan letter.

In fact, "Aunt Clara's Correspondence"
is one of my all-time favorites
of the poems we've published.

I found Aunt Clara's voice irresistible .
I know that lovely voice very well.
I love to have her correspondence

for *SUBTROPICS*.

All the best to you.

Sidney wade
Poetry Editor
SUBTROPICS

(B)

KRINGLA / Found Poem from Patsy and Mayor Mike Jensen

—to Reuben and Clara Nibe, their son, Herb, his daughter, Patsy

Mike: I am forwarding a note from Patsy to you on Kringla—
      see below.

Patsy: Wow! Thanks for the generous complement, but I hardly feel
      like a Kringla expert, it's just that I make so many. I have
      always used Grandma Clara's recipe, it's never failed me.
      But my goodness, I could never compete with Story City
      matriarchs Dorothy Peter or Bertina Frette. Gracious.

      Anyway, here's Grandma Clara's recipe:

KRINGLA

1 stick margarine
1 cup sugar
1 egg
2 tsp baking powder
1 & ½ tsp baking soda
2 cups thick buttermilk—mix alternately with
3 & ½ cups flour until slightly firm but still sticky
(grandma writes, "more" or "less").
Chill. (I chill overnight in refrigerator)>
Next day, form into figure 8s or Qs or Os.
(Do not use too much flour or bake too long)
As for size of the kringla, I think it is six of one
and half dozen of the other, you do what you feel
comfortable and how the finished product looks.
Bake in hot oven till dough is "formed"
then broil to slightly brown kringla on top.
Enjoy hot with butter or peanut butter
like Herb always did!!! Wouldn't Grandma Clara
just shake her head and wonder, "What's all the fuss?"

Mike: That is it. GOOD LUCK AND
        A MERRY CHRISTMAS TO ALL !!!!!!!!!!!!!
(B)

ABOUT THE POETS

Barry Benson has taught English and writing from 8th grade through community college, written news and feature stories for a weekly newspaper, and served as co-poetry editor (with Jody Speer) of a literary journal, *Stand Alone*. His poems are published in journals such as *Subtropics, North American Review, Plainsongs, Flyway, Spoon River Poetry Review, Terminus, Mid-American Poetry Review, Nassau Review, Comstock Review, Timber Creek Review, Brevities, The Iconoclast, Hidden Oak, Briar Cliff Review*, and others. He lives in Des Moines.

Steve Benson, a fourth generation Iowan, studied poetry with James Hearst at the University of Northern Iowa where he started out as a football-playing art major. He taught art in public schools, grades 1 through 12, for over 30 years. His poems have appeared in such literary journals as *The North American Review, MARGIE, Poet Lore, The Briar Cliff Review, Bryant Literary Review, Spoon River Poetry Review, Plainsongs, South Carolina Review, The MacGuffin, The Minnesota Review, Wisconsin Review*, and *The Hollins Critic*. Twenty of his poems have been published by *The Christian Science Monitor*. In 2003, seven of his poems were included in *The Dryland Fish: An Anthology of Contemporary Iowa Poets*. His chapbook, *A Light in the Kitchen*, was the winner of The 2001 Blue Light Poetry Prize. He lives with his wife and children in Mt. Vernon, Iowa.

Printed in the United States of America

www.ingramcontent.com/pod-product-compliance
Lightning Source LLC
Chambersburg PA
CBHW022009090426
42741CB00007B/954

9 781421 837284